JAPANESE GARDENS FOR

TODAY by David H. Engel

with a foreword by RICHARD NEUTRA

CHARLES E. TUTTLE COMPANY : PUBLISHERS
RUTLAND, VERMONT   TOKYO, JAPAN

Representatives

For Continental Europe:
BOXERBOOKS, INC., Zurich

For the British Isles:
PRENTICE-HALL INTERNATIONAL, INC., London

For Canada:
HURTIG PUBLISHERS, Edmonton

For Australasia:
BOOK WISE (AUSTRALIA) PTY. LTD.
104-108 Sussex Street, Sydney 2000

Published by the
Charles E. Tuttle Company, Inc.,
of Rutland, Vermont & Tokyo, Japan
with editorial offices at
Suido 1-chome, 2-6, Bunkyo-ku, Tokyo

Copyright in Japan, 1959
by Charles E. Tuttle Co., Inc.

Library of Congress
Catalog Card No. 59-8191

International Standard Book No. 0-8048-0301-3

First edition, 1959
Tenth printing, 1978

Book design & typography: M. Weatherby

Manufactured in Japan

DEDICATED TO
DAVID AND STELLA ENGEL
AND TO
TANSAI SANO

Table of Contents

List of Illustrations

Foreword

by Richard Neutra, F. A. I. A.

A GENERATION ago, when I accepted my first invitation from Japan to express my ideas on a biological, naturalistic approach to design, upon arriving there I suddenly felt as if I were coming home. And so do I feel now when I read the pages of this book and look at its wonderfully telling pictures of garden art and nature near places for living.

Stronger and livelier becomes my conviction that nature is the great antecedent of all our satisfactions. This has been so for many thousands of years. Man made infinite and subtle adaptations to nature long before his more gross, and often quickly invented and promoted, artificialities began to fill his field of vision. Now the din and jam of a controversial civilization overwhelm all our senses and our nervous being. In this respect, long-insular Japan is a significant, almost tragic illustration of—and certainly also an argument against—our vaunted "progress." As a matter of fact, we do not have progress, but millions of progresses, fast moving and rebounding from each other's fenders. We seem to live in the midst of collisions, and are stuck at the approach to the celebrated "freeway."

Whenever and wherever I have taxed my brain as a planning consultant—be it in various parts of so gloriously "progressive" Africa, in the South Seas, in tropical America south of Panama, or at the foot of old Mount Ararat ("newly shod" by a busy Turkish-American display of civilization designed to impress Soviet border patrols)—the endless theme of my worry has been the combat between the seemingly "practical" that now arrogantly litters and engulfs the scene and what is "biologically bearable." Survival is a matter of "biorealism." Nothing is more practical than to live and wholesomely to survive. We are and will remain in need of nature. But nature pure and simple, untouched nature, is, of course, a lost paradise to man. The people of Tokyo—along with those of Brooklyn, Sao Paulo, Calcutta, Johannesburg—have all been expelled from the primeval scene and crowded into a dense jumble of today's shiny novelties and rusty leftovers from yesterday's crop of quick-turnover products.

Japanese Gardens for Today is a memento against shallow and fast change. Leaving aside the matter of ritual symbolism, I have always felt the Japanese garden to be a design in time as well as in space. In it, the eternity of shape is kept before our soul by many laborious but rewarding hours of inconspicuous maintenance. In its volumes and in its space relations a twelfth-century garden looks today just as it did hundreds of years ago, although it is composed, not of mummies and relics, but largely of living plants. This is a time cult; it points to the significance time has to life.

Though in different, contrasting ways to this perpetual "still picture" presented by a Japanese garden, the twin-shrine of Ise, one of the holiest centers of

Japan's native religion, demonstrates and dramatizes *time*. There one of the two identical sanctuaries is always under construction, while the other, being used for worship, casts a side glance at its own mirror-image rejuvenation nearby. And once in every generation the intangible godhead of the shrine is transferred from the old to the new building in solemn ritual. After this the old building is demolished and the rebuilding begun again. It is a ritual demonstration, conscious or unconscious, of the never-ending process of decay and renewal that runs through all eternity.

Built and jointed as it is with wonderful neatness and solidity, there is no "practical" need to tear down the shrine. It is not obsolete. It might well stand for a thousand years. Likewise, there is no practical reason for tending a garden so that through the centuries it will always present, statically, the same compositional ideas. The rationale of what happens both at the Ise Shrine and in the Japanese garden is the same—a symbolic linking of time before the soul of man. Fashion does not penetrate here; an uncanny force of primary design, seeming to embody the stability of nature itself, fends off fatigue, neither tiring man nor boring him.

The universal, balanced ecology of Kruger Park in the Transvaal and American primeval settings, in the midst of which I have been privileged to invest creative effort, are next to eternal, as also are the nature preserves of the Belgian Congo and Brazil; their wonderful lasting balance has an overpowering impressiveness. So too does the Japan garden continue to symbolize these long-range values of equilibrium, even while there flows outside its moon gate a thickening parade of two-toned, chrome-trimmed motor cars of the very latest fashions, blowing ephemeral exhaust fumes.

David H. Engel points in his text to the mystery of how traditional Japanese houses fuse with their gardens, gardens so spontaneously free of the shackles of dry geometricity. The house, on the contrary, could well serve American prefabricators as prototype solutions of the problems of modular construction, as an example of a most humanized standardization accepted by a hundred million people. The three-by-six-foot *tatami* floor mat governs not only the dimensions of a room, whose size is always some multiple of the mat, but also those of the sliding partitions of the house, the built-in sets of drawers, the movable *tansu* chests—governs, indeed, every dimension of houses at every level of society, from the huts of poor farmers to the palatial villas of soap manufacturers and princely officials.

The original quality which flows from these ever-cherished building standards harmonizes amazingly well with the relaxed asymmetry of the garden courtyard, and probably needs it for instinctive relief. "Humanized naturalism," as I, like Mr. Engel, would call it, demands this kind of partnership. It becomes more than mere partnership and turns into a true *entity*, an almost puzzling integration with the site, which is respected as part of the continuous universe —before this universe was marred by commercially developed "subdivisions." It is amazing how all this outwardly related unity can be accomplished even on the most diminished scale, where vistas could never hope to be as expansive as in the Mikado's summer palace. Japanese gardens have made happy the humble, the modest, and the rich.

Mr. Engel agrees with my long-harbored thoughts. All our senses are used in apprehending a designed setting, be it architecture or landscaping. Even the vestibular sense of the inner ear busily records for us our turns, accelerations, and retardations when, following a magical paving pattern, we haltingly walk the irregular windings of a carefully planned, non-repetitious path or tread the willful zigzag of simple planks bridging a lotus pool.

Thus, a visitor to such a jewel of gardening is kept, with brilliant foresight, tenderly activated by the multi-sensorial appeal of the sounds, odors, and colors of nature, the thermal variations of shade, sunlight, and air movements. Happy endocrine discharges and pleasant associations play through the visitor's body and mind as he views and promenades. Or, even when he sits seemingly in full repose, that strangely emotive "force of form" that exists in the garden keeps eliciting the vital, vibrating functions of the subtle life processes within him that we call

delight. All this is far beyond the effects worked on us by merely quaint, exotic decoration.

The author of this valuable book rightly warns against its being used superficially for the shallow imitation of fragments. The book's greatest benefit will be to stir an awakening to the unified appeal that results from such a profoundly integrated composition as a Japanese garden. This same principle of total appeal has also been practiced, often with completely unstudied innocence, from neolithic Machu Picchu in the precipitous mountains of Peru to Zulu villages in the African bush, but it has, alas, all but disappeared where our herds of bulldozers have bullied the landscape into a "marketable" product.

Japanese towns, villages, houses, and gardens are often miracles of land economy, brought about both out of necessity and from a general sense of thrift. This book gives much more than a glimpse of the "humanized naturalism" of the Japanese landscape, a landscape that proves that even a tightly massed civilization need not spell the defilement of the natural scene but, in fact, can mean its glorification.

Los Angeles, February, 1959

Acknowledgments

It is always a pleasant task to thank those who have helped you. In this instance it can truly be said that it was the encouragement and generous assistance of many Japanese well-wishers that brought this book into being. Though it would be impossible to list them all, I shall never forget the many friendly, open doors of private homes and temples where I was always so cordially received. No matter how busy they were, housewives, homeowners, and temple priests were proud and happy to invite me inside, to show their houses and gardens, and to talk to me over a hospitable, warming cup of tea.

There are also those to whom I must especially express my gratitude. First, to Tansai Sano, artist, garden designer, and builder. He is a humble man of taste and sensitivity who, while deeply loving the rich heritage of his country's culture, still does not hesitate to try, with bright, creative originality, new forms of artistic expression in a garden. He is my teacher and my friend. With enthusiasm he accepted me as his pupil. With gentle humor and patience he listened to my questions. And he taught me not only principles of garden design and construction, but also to see gardens as a joyful part of the human adventure.

I am also grateful to the Landscape Architecture Department of the Faculty of Agriculture of Kyoto University for the use of its well-stocked library. I am deeply indebted to Professor Eitaro Sekiguchi and his staff, and especially to Makoto Nakamura, who helped me with his friendly criticism and advice.

I am thankful also to the Faculty of Architecture of Tokyo University of Fine Arts, where I was registered; to Professor Junzo Yoshimura, who smoothed the way; to Professor Isoya Yoshida; and to Gakuji Yamamoto, for his encouraging and helpful letters.

As indicated below, for many of the photographs in this book I am obliged to Seiichi Sano, who is following in his father's distinguished tradition of garden building, and to Yoshio Takahashi, who spent almost two years photographing gardens all over Japan for the publishing house of Kodansha.

The staff of the City of Kyoto's Bureau of Tourist Industry were most helpful and cooperative in securing for me introductions and passes to many of the gardens. And, above all, with fondness and gratitude my appreciation goes to my friend Eiko Yuasa, of that office, who typed the manuscript for me and in countless hospitable, generous ways helped me during my stay in Japan. I thank my friend Kiyoshi Makino, the Tokyo architect, who allowed me to use the pictures of the Sassakawa, designed by him.

To Hiroshi Uemura, garden designer and builder in Kanazawa, who gave so generously of his time and whose name unlocked many a garden gate, I feel grateful obligation.

My thanks to Tadashi Kubo, of the Agricultural Faculty of Osaka Prefectural University, who sent me his compilation of the *Sakutei-ki*. For their help with many of the drawings I am obliged to Shiotaro Shizuma and Shigeo Fujita.

I owe gratitude to the Japanese government, which awarded me, through its Ministry of Education, a grant to study garden design and construction in Japan.

And to the Japan Society in New York, which helped me to get started on this study project, I am most grateful.

The gardens of Messrs. Tomoda, Mizoguchi, Kaba, Watanabe, Tamura, and Ishida and of the Narita Fudo and the Kicho, illustrated in pages which follow, were designed and built by Tansai Sano. The garden of Mr. Akaza was designed and built by Hiroshi Uemura.

The sources of the photographs used in the book are as follows, all those not otherwise indicated having been taken by the author:

By Seiichi Sano: Plates 1, 3, 19, 20, 28, 31, 37, 42, 43, 45, 48–50, 52–55, 59, 60, 63–67, 70, 78–80, 102–5, 112, 113, 121, 125, 127, 130–32, 135, 137, 139, 144, 146, 148, 154–56, 159, 161–63, 166, 176, 177, 181, 182, 184, 185, 187–89, 198, 202, 205, 207–9, 223, 232, 234, 236, and 265; and Color Plates 6–7 and 10.

By Yoshio Takahashi, and used by courtesy of Kodansha, Tokyo: Color Plates 1–3, 5, 9, 11, and 15.

Courtesy of the Bureau of Tourist Industry, Kyoto: Plates 72, 76, 97, and 193.

Courtesy of Kiyoshi Makino: Plates 24–25.

DAVID H. ENGEL

Japanese Gardens for Today

Introduction

SWIRLING out of the Japanese garden a fresh concept of design is running strongly through today's landscape architecture. This lively current forms part of the broad stream of ideas emanating from the Orient and especially from Japan's seemingly inexhaustible wells of art. In the past few years Occidental architecture and design have been subjected to steady contact through such extensive importation of Far Eastern influences that at times they have appeared to be almost inundated. The responsibility of pointing out the misinterpretations, downright fads, and nonsense in the "Japanese trend" rests with the designers and architects. It remains, of course, for each artistic discipline to study new ideas and practices, to guard against the introduction of the tasteless and irrelevant, and to select from the mass of things what is valid and beautiful.

For landscape architecture and garden design, then, this book is intended to serve as a guide on the subject of Japanese gardens. It shows many kinds of gardens as illustrations of design principles. Its immediate purpose is to provide both professional landscape architects and amateur garden builders with a handbook to help them in their work. The aim here is to stimulate the imagination and to suggest a challenge.

The scope of the book differs from previous works on Japanese gardens in that it neither offers general and abstruse esthetic critiques and interpretations of famous Japanese gardens nor does it delve into their religious, romantic, and historical associations —though in their place these too are fascinating.

The Japanese garden is treated here, not as a quaint, exotic, Oriental bird, but as a living, artistic structure with important significance for people in countries outside of Japan.

The book is the product of on-the-spot research and study and the practical experience of working with a master garden artist—an apprenticeship in design, construction, and plant care—extending over almost two years in Kyoto and other parts of Japan.

Today's widespread interest in garden art is a healthy sign. But of even more significance is the fact that it is the Japanese garden which is causing much of the ferment. Thus there is evidence not only of evolution in the field—a search for better forms in landscape design—but also of rejection, perhaps on both subconscious and conscious levels, of materialistic principles in gardening and landscaping. It may be that this heralds an awakening to the need for gardens which can stimulate responses that spring from our innermost recesses.

The paradox of the mid-twentieth century is that, while the material advantages and luxuries produced by modern technology encompass us and touch all aspects of our lives, we have had the uneasy feeling of being uprooted, of losing contact with nature, of "getting soft." We cannot stem the tide of technology —and perhaps do not even want to. Yet, almost instinctively feeling the need to put down roots in a natural setting, we have moved to *Suburbia* and beyond to *Exurbia*. Architects, both of houses and of gardens, have recognized the extent and depth of the necessity to "get back to nature." Witness the contemporary design of homes and gardens which are built for so-called "indoor-outdoor living."

We may at times succeed in the attempt at integrating house and garden, hoping thereby to achieve a kind of harmonious relationship with nature. More often, however, we have missed the point because of our reliance upon a narrowly materialistic, functional approach. It is at that point that we can learn from the Japanese.

Living close to nature is the very essence of life in Japan. The Japanese makes little distinction between nature and deity. His house and garden then seem the perfect cradle, for there he feels closer to his God. House and garden represent the happy marriage of art and nature, and one can barely distinguish a dividing line at which the house ends and the garden begins.

When the concept of the thin line that separates architecture and nature is discussed outside of Japan the point is often raised that the especially close relationship between house and garden might be all very well for Japan. "But," it is asked, "are Japanese gardens functional in America, in Europe? They may work under Japanese conditions but can their principles be applied outside Japan?"

The answer is that, of course, no one advocates merely copying the Japanese garden. What *is* proposed is simply that we understand the principles of its design, its handling of materials, and, above all, its spirit. Once having grasped these essentials, we may proceed to plan a garden, adapting the sense and spirit of Japanese design to the material and physical requirements and limitations of the project.

Indeed, the concept of functionalism has a spiritual as well as a material aspect. Though in recent times it has become a cliché in our daily life, functionalism certainly is neither a new discovery nor does the term indicate an advanced mode of living. It is true, of course, that all that functions in a Japanese setting may not necessarily work favorably outside of Japan. Yet the West, which has become so engrossed in the material aspects of "functional living," may well profit from an appreciation of what a functional garden means to a Japanese. A simple garden of a Japanese home from which the members of the family derive pleasure as they view it through each season of the year surely serves some functional purpose *(see, for example, the gardens of Plates 1, 35, 37, 51 and 56).* To be sure, the garden has no barbecue grill, swimming pool, or play area, but it does convey, past the open, paper-panelled *shoji* and across the grass mat *tatami* threshold, a sense of repose and identification with nature's own harmony. Could not an Occidental garden inducing the same effect also be considered functional? This, of course, is not to say that the way to mental health or peace of mind and soul leads necessarily through a Japanese garden. But rather I suggest only that the meditative, receptive element be recognized as most desirable and that it be combined in appropriate proportions with active, exertive enjoyment of a garden.

The organic form of a Japanese garden, as of a Western garden, depends upon the basic type of building it is designed for—a small private house in town, a hotel or inn, a teahouse, a restaurant, a

Color Plate 1. A pond often forms a central element of Japanese garden design. In the pond seen here, the water level has dropped ten inches, temporarily revealing the rocky shoreline that is normally under water (see Color Plate 12). Each rock rests on its own rock piling sunk into the clayey bank. The low shoreline and peninsula in the foreground has a sunken rock bed over which are laid small rounded black stones. Note how the rocks are arranged as promontories and inlets of a real ocean shoreline, some jutting out into the water and some receding into coves. (Katsura Imperial Villa, Kyoto.)

Color Plate 2. A view of the type of pond called *shinji-ike*, i.e., a pond in the form of the Chinese character *shin*, meaning "heart, soul, spirit," a favorite character with the Zen sect of Buddhism. The light filtering through the trees and the softness of the moss-covered earth invite meditation. This garden is the work of Muso Kokushi, a famous Zen priest of the fourteenth century. (Saiho-ji, Kyoto.)

large country villa, a mansion, palace, or temple. Styles reflect individual taste, local tradition, foreign influences, and changes in the economic and social structure of Japanese society. But despite differences in form and style a good Japanese garden invariably reveals three fundamental characteristics: naturalism, asymmetry, and a drawing together of natural and architectural forms into a unified, harmonious composition. It is a work of art, built on a human scale, naturalistic in content but subjective in spirit.

Conscious and keen observation and appreciation of wild nature inspires the creator of a Japanese garden. In executing his design, however, the raw forms of nature are symbolized, suggested, implied. The garden-maker's objective is to humanize the natural landscape immediately around him, not to force it into a strait-jacket of bilateral symmetry; he aims, with artistry and discrimination, to select out of nature those elements that he feels are most perfect and pertinent to his composition. This is what is meant when it is said that the Japanese garden is subjective in spirit.

The materials of the Japanese garden are selected to bring the timelessness and solidity of the world of nature into a garden. Thus, lasting elements such as rock, gravel, sand, and evergreen trees and shrubs are predominant, while fleeting blossoms and color play the counterpoint. This has been a distinctive attribute of Japanese gardens for eight centuries, ever since the Kamakura period, when Zen Buddhist meditation, though demanding freedom *from* the world's bright, gaudy distractions, still insisted upon a feeling *for* the world. Under such conditions the garden became an idealization of nature in which could be discovered something of the heart of nature, of its very elemental spirit. It was designed so that the beholder could relate himself to nature. By discovering in it something of ordinary human experience he felt drawn into the garden and even a part of it. This very subjective experience is an expression of the all-embracing Buddhist concept of the oneness, the unity of all things under Heaven.

Such feeling bears little relation to certain popular notions of Japanese gardens flourishing outside Japan. These stereotypes have been propagated and nourished by three generations of visitors, who, over the past one hundred years, have periodically "discovered" Japan. In the big cities these visitors may catch a glimpse of gardens of teahouses and restaurants in all their overdone, cluttered ornamentation. From this fleeting contact they believe the Japanese garden to be a quaint, tinkling medley of little arched bridges, carp ponds, paper lanterns, oddly pruned trees, bamboo blinds, grotesquely jutting rocks, and perhaps a dainty geisha. Other travelers, who barely get beyond Tokyo's Imperial Hotel lobby and gift shops, have conceived of the Japanese garden to have something to do with dwarfed plants and the miniatures of a tray landscape. Many visitors, of course, do make the regular tours of Nikko, Kyoto, and Nara to view those cities' celebrated temples, shrines, palaces, and gardens. They may see famous feudal-period gardens, built on a grand scale, of imposing richness and intricate detail. But many of these are also sadly artificial and sterile, having no relationship to the life of the common man, devoid of the bright buoyancy of nature. Visitors to these places come away convinced that Japanese gardens must be filled with giant stone lanterns and great rocks and boulders.

The problem is that, even with only superficial contact with Japanese gardens, the outsider is bound to form an opinion of garden art in Japan. The average traveler, unfortunately, sees nothing but the external decorative elements. He has not had the chance to see either simple, well-designed, modern home gardens or very old ones made in the earlier and more creative periods of Japanese garden art. Diverted by exotic and romantic elements, most visitors to Japan have missed the real point of a Japanese garden. It surely is not merely a matter of using rocks, pebbles, unpainted wood surfaces, Japanese maples, twisted pines, rocky pools, waterfalls, garden rills, bridges, pagodas, stone lanterns, or Buddhas. The elements of the Japanese garden are not just dramatic garden props, used for easy upkeep and unique effect. If it were so, the garden would be merely a clutter of things, sterile, insincere, false. Above all, a good garden has naturalness, strength, simplicity, humor, and human warmth. Its elements are arranged to convey the feeling of the partnership of nature and art. In effect, the symbolism is that of man and nature in a pact of friendship, sealing it, as it were, with a hearty handshake.

You do not have to be a lover of Japanese culture to be able to grasp some strong validity in its garden art. From the standpoint of pure design it is logical and honest. But, more than that, its bonds are stronger and its roots deeper than any we have known heretofore in the realm of garden art. They are ties of an ineffable spirituality, which can be felt at all levels of perception. And this forms what may be the real attraction of Japanese gardens at this critical juncture of Western cultural growth.

PART ONE

The Theory:

1. Some Universal Garden Effects

WE ARE children of nature. But since the dawn of life we have come a good distance. Our human civilization down through the years has evolved into ever more intricate and complex urban patterns, in which steel and concrete have come to play the predominant role. Though it seems obvious that at least one foot is irretrievably stuck in the hard city pavement, the other remains just as solidly planted in the moist, soft earth. We will never give up loving nature, wanting some quiet, beneficent refuge to go back to when the "world is too much with us." And so we have made gardens.

A garden offers us security. It is as if a kind power instilled in a garden has come around to preserve us. We do not, of course, respond to all manifestations of nature with indiscriminate trust and open arms. From the very beginning we have made the distinction between nature in the raw and the humanized landscape. In the midst of untamed wildernesses of forests, mountains, plains, swamps, deserts, tundra, or jungle we are struck with awe by the power and majesty of nature expressed in great stretches of uncultivated terrain, untouched or ungentled by man.

Such feelings are altogether different from what we experience in a pleasant spring meadow surrounded by the sights and smells and sounds of farm life. Or, lying under an apple tree whose fragrant blossoms pour out their perfume into the burgeoning spring air, we feel some upsurging energy, a link with nature's creative drive. Any bit of humanized landscape, whether it be large or small, elaborate or simple, used for flowers, fruit, vegetables, or grazing, has qualities of a garden; and, as such, can be enjoyed in varying degrees and ways according to our special interests, experience, and sensitivity.

But, although a farm may offer us nature in a humanized setting, we know that a farm and a garden are not the same thing. The former is designed with a view to the practical requirements of an efficiently producing agricultural unit; while the latter is made, not for economic gain, but with a view to esthetic values and to serve a purpose offering no direct economic or material benefits. The value of a well-designed garden may be judged only by the subjective effects it produces on the people who use it. It might be an effect of pleasure caused by some esthetic perception; an effect of convenience, leisure, or repose induced by some direct sensory experience in the garden; an effect of spiritual enrichment, the result of some mystic inspirational process; or, depending upon the individual, the time, and the place, it might be combinations of all of these effects in varying proportions and strengths. It is evident then that while the appeal of a garden is universal, the effects it may produce depend upon its location and its particular individual character. The latter is in turn the product of local tradition, customs, and the way the garden was designed to be used. The personality of the user is the final determinant.

What, then, are those desirable garden effects that have pleased men in all times and all places? Let us consider them in the following paragraphs.

Space & Vista. We love the effect of spaciousness and vista. Looking across long, unrestricted distances, we gain a feeling of freedom. As we gaze at a far horizon our imagination takes flight. But we also like our privacy.

Of course, if our garden is located in a sparsely populated area, such as desert, mountain, seashore, or woods, we may be able to combine both vista and privacy. A home perched on a hillside or mountaintop gets complete privacy as well as a mountain view. *(See Plate 2.)* These days, homes are being built on the edges and even in the midst of the American desert. The sand and rock, mountain and basin, of the desert, in all its changing moods and colors, enter into the garden design and become a part of it. And probably this is what the people who live there like most about their environment. They moved to the desert to gain both privacy and a view.

Privacy. In other instances, a sense both of space and vista and of privacy are mutually exclusive. If we gain one, we lose the other. Anyone with a garden in an urban or semi-urban area, where houses are relatively close together, and who insists on freedom to enjoy his house and garden as he pleases, will require some kind of enclosure. Fences limit his view but substitute for it a sense of personal freedom. This is certainly a desirable effect that becomes necessary as we live more and more in our "outside room." It is, in fact, more democratic to put up a wall, fence, hedge, or plant screen than to live constantly within the sight and sound of our neighbors. With no privacy in our garden we feel constrained and inhibited by

Color Plate 3. Nature and art met here six hundred years ago when this garden was first created. Since then, the trees have passed through more than one generation of planting. Through the high overhead limbs the light filters through to the ground, providing the partial shade that is the perfect condition for the moss that now holds sway. But the hand of man, though ever so lightly applied, is still at the controls. (View from Koin-zan, Saiho-ji, Kyoto.)

Color Plate 4. This is not a wild, wooded glade. It is a gentle landscape constructed about six hundred years ago as a "stroll garden" for a temple built at the foot of a wooded hill. The groundcover is moss of many species, which long ago took over from the rocks set in the banks of the pond and along its paths. The trees are principally pines, maples, and evergreen oaks interspersed with spring-flowering trees and shrubs and bamboo. (Saiho-ji, Kyoto.)

fears of annoying our neighbors or of incurring their disapproval. But by simply erecting a barrier the problem is solved. Each may now live his life as he sees fit, with no interference from or disturbance of the people next door. Enclosure also induces a pleasing effect of repose and tranquillity by cutting out distracting outside noises and sights *(see Plate 3).* Finally, it defines the limits of a garden, just as a frame sets off a painting, thereby enhancing its beauty.

Age & Antiquity. A sense of age and antiquity is another garden effect. We love to feel that things embody tradition and continuity with the past. We thereby gain roots. It is an assumption of dignity and substance, of a well-established place in our society. We treasure our antiques. An old house or a venerable landmark evokes a kind of nostalgia in us. We have the feeling that we would like to live there, if not to possess it. *(See Plates 175, 187, 188, 194, and 197.)*

Rhythm of Nature. We see the imperishable, the neverending rhythm of nature manifested in the elemental forces which are always at work even in the most insignificant details of a garden. Thus, after a long, cold winter we are reassured of nature's power and cyclic beat on first seeing the tender buds of the crocus pushing their heads up through the residual snows of March and April. It is a promise of the renewal of the seasons. Equally heartening is the feeling we experience standing in a grove of California's giant redwood sequoia, listening to the wind sighing through the towering treetops.

Imagination. A garden which stirs the imagination has precious vitality. This effect requires that everything not be revealed to complete view from any single vantage point. The spectator is left to imagine what lies behind a hedge, a turn of the path masked by an artful arrangement of shrubs and rocks, the winding thread of a murmuring brook whose banks can be only partially seen from any one point in the garden, a lake whose shoreline is indented by rocky inlets, or the depths of a woodland glade, dark and shady in some parts and light and sunny in others *(see Plates 4 and 12).*

In quite another way the imagination may be stirred through the perception of materials in the garden, formed into abstract designs, or, on a small scale, made to symbolize grand features of the natural landscape *(see Plates 11 and 87).*

2. Some Human Principles

A STROLL in a garden affects our senses of touch, sight, sound, and smell. The sense of touch is affected by feelings of muscular activity and memories of tactile sensations. So is it also with sound and sight and smell, recalling memories from the past. These sensations stimulate perceptions, which then lead on to the formation of intellectual concepts. These three compose the materials of our imagination. The pleasure of a sensation is determined by its duration, intensity, and character. We derive pleasure from perception by discovering esthetic harmonies and unities, while pleasure in intellection arises from relating our concepts.

Any design to be successful must stimulate recognition of the universality of experience. This applies to gardens as well as to other works of art. A successful garden then must satisfy certain needs felt by the people who use it. These needs are for logical, economic, esthetic, and spiritual unity. They require the presentation of truth, the satisfaction of a physical need, the apprehension of a complete esthetic totality, and finally man's identification with nature and his God.

Logical Unity. We love to look at things that are logical, the reflections of truth, and the realities of our environment and daily lives. We respect sincerity and abhor falseness. We appreciate what we can understand and feel and know, but we hate to be fooled. We want genuine things about us. If we have to choose between artificial roses, no matter how beautifully and artfully they are contrived, and a bed of modest violets, we would still prefer the latter. We reject sham and look for what is real.

Economic Unity. When we seek the satisfaction of a physical need we are simply choosing what we can put to use. This is economic unity which is easily grasped. We tend to select what makes sense and has for us some practical value, and we discard the senseless and useless. Thus, for example, a young family needs a simple garden where the growing children can play without the parents' worrying that they are ruining the garden and with the least risk of injury to the children. In such circumstances a fish pond or intricate flower and shrubbery arrangements would be disastrous. Or, a retired couple who love to work in their garden need a place which will challenge their creative energies, providing a happy way to pass the time that hangs heavy in retirement. Physical needs vary with the individual, but a good garden that satisfies these needs, whatever they be, has economic unity.

Esthetic Unity. We want our garden also to have esthetic unity. It must be a composition that affords pleasure in the beholding because we can immediately appreciate, consciously or unconsciously, harmonious relations in the color, texture, shape, size, attitudes, and intervals of its parts. Stated subjectively, it is a harmony of interest and not merely of objects or characteristics.

If a garden has logical and economic unity but not esthetic unity, it is not a real garden. Art is the missing factor. Design, of course, is not hard and fast. It varies with each project which has its own conditions—the objective ones of the site and the subjective ones of the people who will live on it. In his book *Landscape for Living*, Garrett Eckbo recognizes how esthetic unity may be captured when he writes:

"Our theory then must point the way to good form in the landscape; but it cannot define it rigidly, on an exclusive, selected basis, with dogma and formulae, rules and regulations, precedents and measured drawings. We must base ourselves upon a flexible understanding and assimilation of those basic questions of scale, proportion, unity, variety, rhythm, repetition, which have been the primary guides for good men in all fields in all times and places."

Spiritual Unity. Going one step further, granted that a garden has logical, economic, and esthetic unity, if it still lacks a spiritual unity, it has not achieved its final and best purpose. This is the unity which ties the building to its natural environment, and then links the people who live there to both. It means that in the course of living in our house and garden we become a part of it, and it a part of us. This is the unique quality, the ideal of a Japanese garden.

3. Some Intrinsic Characteristics

THE INTERACTION of primary geographical and cultural factors accounts for the development of Japan's unique arts and especially its gardens. Because Japan is an archipelago of generally mountainous terrain located in the northern latitudes and surrounded by warm ocean currents, it has abundant rainfall, heavy growth of forests, and a temperate climate with pronounced changes from season to season. And, because a small sea separates Japan from the mainland of Asia, its own native folkways were long allowed to develop relatively untouched by outside influences. But, though isolated from the rest of Asia, it was never completely inaccessible. As a result, Japan's early culture of primitive animism and nature worship underwent great changes under the impact of the introduction of the sophistication of China and Korea. Through the synthesis of Japan's native traditions and customs with vigorous Chinese and Korean intellectual, artistic, and religious teachings there developed a new and fuller Japanese culture which attained great subtlety, refinement, and spiritual depth. The strongest influence of all was Buddhism.

The Buddhist religion itself had felt the formative effects of Confucian and Taoist ideals and philosophy as it passed through China in the long journey from India to Japan. And, within the world of Buddhism, it was the sect of Zen that left the deepest impression on Japanese art. From this penetrating contact emerged the spiritual concept of man's partnership with nature. This concept became the hallmark of Japanese painting, architecture, literature, and, not least, of Japanese gardens. We shall term this humanized naturalism.

Humanized Naturalism. Partnership with nature requires that man and nature be on very familiar terms. Thus, the Japanese artist went out to study nature in all its varied forms. He examined it at close-up and from afar so that while executing his art he was able to visualize all aspects of nature under all conditions in all seasons. The very nature of this process however, meant that what the artist could give was always his subjective interpretation. The garden artist too could never merely copy nature. The naturalness of Japanese gardens became an essence of some aspect of nature, modest or grand, interpreted by the garden artist as his impression of real nature. In this process his deep reverence for nature was implicit.

Partnership and familiarity with nature soon revealed to the garden artist several artistic truths. He saw that the over-all impression one receives from nature is one of strong asymmetry. Though in minute details, such as the arrangement of a flower's stamen and pistil, the shape of a leaf, or snow crystals, nature might be symmetrical, still the larger view of nature revealed just the opposite. This observation became a principle of design of the landscape garden, but

Color Plate 5. The off-white gravel groundcover provides an astringent contrast with the bright reds of the autumn foliage and the soft, dark tones of the rocks and evergreen plantings. (Shugaku-in Imperial Villa, Kyoto.)

Color Plates 6 & 7. This is the prospect that greets you when you pass through the street gate into the front garden of this private residence. The walk is of three-inch-thick granite slabs set in a bed of sand, with dry, hairline joints. The straightforward formality of the pattern of the walk is offset by the abstract shape of the gravel "pool," the natural rocks set in and around its shoreline, the moss groundcover, and the shrub plantings. Since this picture was taken shortly after the garden was completed, the moss had not yet taken hold and spread its deep green cover. Plant materials used here are cryptomeria, Japanese andromeda, Japanese maple, and Japanese holly. Designed by Tansai Sano. (Toyoda residence, Juso, Osaka Prefecture.)

here nature's violent asymmetry became tamed and balanced by the humanism of man.

The preference for asymmetry was encouraged by Taoist and Zen teachings which intellectualized it as an element of Japanese esthetics. In *The Book of Tea* Kakuzo Okakura called his country's art the "abode of the unsymmetrical." Contrasting Western and Asian approaches to design, he pointed out how the Taoist-Zen conception of perfection differed from that of the West. The dynamic nature of Taoist and Zen philosophies "laid more stress upon the process through which perfection was sought than upon perfection itself. True beauty could be discovered only by one who mentally completed the incomplete. The virility of life and art lay in its possibilities for growth. In the tea-room (as in the garden) it is left for each guest in imagination to complete the total effect in relation to himself. Since Zen has become the prevailing mode of thought, the art of the Far East has purposely avoided bilateral symmetry as expressing not only completion but repetition. Uniformity of design was considered as fatal to the freshness of imagination. Thus, landscapes, birds and flowers became the favorite subjects for depiction rather than the human figure, the latter being present in the person of the beholder himself."

In another passage Okakura advised the artist to leave something unsaid so that the beholder be given the chance "to complete the idea. Thus a great masterpiece irresistibly rivets your attention until you seem to become actually a part of it. A vacuum is there for you to enter and fill up to the full measure of your esthetic emotion."

This humanized naturalism of which we are speaking has a further human element in that, though a Japanese garden is basically naturalistic, it by no means is restricted to the use of nothing but natural forms. But, when geometrical, man-made shapes are used, they serve as a foil to frame and set off the elements of purely naturalistic form. For example, the straight line of a clipped hedge or a path of geometrically shaped steppingstones commonly serves as a contrasting non-naturalistic element. Or, geometrical shapes play an important role as symbols of natural forms. Thus, a bank of rounded, sheared azalea bushes in several sizes and heights, seemingly piled one upon the other in depth, may symbolize mountains. In such a case they are active, humanized substitutes for rock and stone, which, although inert, are also felt to have a life of their own *(see Plate 5)*.

Line & Mass vs. Color. Besides the faithful adherence of the Japanese garden artist to principles of asymmetry, he depends also upon elements of line and mass rather than color to create his landscape design. The unity of the basic structure of the garden is formed by the arrangement of massed evergreen trees and shrubs combined with rocks and artifacts. The prevailing hues are in greens, browns, beiges, and greys, of varying tones. No matter what the season, the main lines and forms remain almost unchanged. The resort to line and mass in garden composition is again, as in the case of asymmetry, only the reproduction in humanized form of what the garden artist has observed in real nature. It is a rare and fleeting phenomenon when color figures importantly in the

Fig. 1. Genji built a garden for Murasaki, his wife. One corner of it may well have looked like this garden belonging to a nobleman of the same time, the Heian period (794–1185). From the picture scroll *Kasuga Gongen Reigen-ki.*

natural landscape of mountains, forests, seacoasts, streams, and fields. Thus, the garden-maker in Japan remains true to nature in adhering to line and mass for the principal structure of his garden, keeping color in a minor role. *(See Plate 6.)*

Genji's Garden.   Color was not always used with such restraint. In a much earlier period of Japanese history, from the eighth to the thirteenth centuries, gardens were open, gay, and filled with flowers and blossoming trees and shrubs as well as all types of water features. They were naturalistic gardens built as idealizations of the real world outside, but more closely resembling the then-prevalent ideas of Heaven. The gardens adorned the palaces and villas of the royal family and wealthy nobles. They contained streams which wound through them to empty into lakes and ponds, which were often large enough to allow shallow-draft, flat-bottomed boats to cruise along their shores. These were boating and excursion gardens, which served as playgrounds for the ranks of the nobility. Islands in the lakes and ponds denoted such Chinese cosmological symbols as *Horai-jima,* the Island of Paradise *(see Plate 96).* Sometimes a line of rocks was laid out in the water, *yodomari-ishi,* to represent ships moored at night in a Chinese harbor *(Plate 98).* Or, one rock projecting out of the water would symbolize *takara-bune,* the treasure ship of Chinese and Japanese legend.

For a picture of those gardens in the Heian period (794–1185) we have the colorful description *(see also Fig. 1)* written over a thousand years ago by Lady Murasaki Shikibu in her novel *The Tale of Genji,* as translated so ably by Arthur Waley:

"Genji effected great improvement in the appearance of the grounds by a judicious handling of knoll and lake, for, though such features were already there in abundance, he found it necessary here to cut away a slope, there to dam a stream, that each occupant of the various quarters might look out of her windows upon such a prospect as pleased her best. To the southeast he raised the level of the ground and on this bank planted a profusion of early flowering trees. At the foot of this slope the lake curved with especial beauty, and in the foreground, just beneath the windows, he planted borders of cinquefoil, of red-plum, cherry, wisteria, kerria, rock-azalea and other such plants as are at their best in springtime...while here and there, in places where they would not obstruct his main plan, autumn beds were cleverly interwoven with the rest.

"Akikonomu's garden was full of such trees as in autumn-time turn to the deepest hue. The stream above the waterfall was cleared out and deepened to a considerable distance; and that the noise of the cascade might carry further, he set great boulders in mid-stream, against which the current crashed and broke. . . .

"In the northeastern garden there was a cool spring, the neighborhood of which seemed likely to yield an agreeable refuge from the summer heat. In the borders near the house upon this side he planted Chinese bamboos, and, a little further off, tall-stemmed forest trees whose thick leaves roofed airy tunnels of shade, pleasant as those of the most lovely upland wood. This garden was fenced with hedges of the white deutzia flower, the orange tree, the briar-rose and the giant peony; with many other sorts of bush and tall flower so skillfully spread about among them that neither spring nor autumn would ever lack in bravery.

". . . Along the stream he planted appropriate purple irises. . . . To the north of Lady Akashi's rooms rose a high embankment, screened by a close-set wall of pine trees, planted there on the purpose that she might have the pleasure of seeing them when their boughs were laden with snow; and for her delight in the earlier days of the winter there was a great bed of chrysanthemums, which he pictured her enjoying on some morning when all the garden was white with frost.

". . . Murasaki's Spring garden seemed to become every day more enchanting. The little wood on the hill beyond the lake, the bridge that joined the two islands, the mossy banks that seemed to grow greener not every day but every hour—could anything have looked more tempting.

". . . The rowers brought them close in under the rocky bank of the channel between the two large islands. . . the shape of every little ledge and crag of stone had been as carefully devised as if a painter had traced them with his brush. Here and there in the distance the topmost boughs of an orchard showed above the mist, so heavily laden with blossoms that it looked as though a bright carpet were spread in mid-air. Far away they could just catch sight of Murasaki's apartments, marked by the deeper green of the willow boughs that swept her courtyards, and by the shimmer of her flowering orchards, which even at this distance seemed to shed their fragrance amid the isles and rocks. In the world outside, the cherry blossom was almost over; but here it seemed to laugh at decay, and around the palace even the wisteria that ran along the covered alleys and porticos was all in bloom, but not a flower past its best; while here, where the boats were tied, mountain-kerria poured its yellow blossom over the rocky cliffs in a torrent of color that was mirrored in the waters of the lake below. . . ."

Reflecting the mood of the court life of the period, those gardens of Genji's were for carefree pleasure for the few who could afford such a life. Deciduous and flowering trees were used in great masses. But as social conditions changed, so did the gardens. By the thirteenth century the gay life of the Heian period had crumbled. The ensuing years of civil war and the appeal of Zen Buddhism's philosophy of simplicity and meditation influenced all branches of the arts. Gardens became more sober and restrained, more impervious to the effects of seasonal change. Evergreen plant materials became predominant.

The Static Quality & Evergreens. The slow, measured, almost drifting tempo of Japanese gardens today is produced by the predominance of slow-growing broad-leaf and needle evergreens combined with rock. Together they form the main structural skeleton of the garden, contrasting with deciduous elements such as maple, cherry, and plum trees, which are generally kept smaller than the evergreen through rigorous and regular pruning. *(See Plate 6.)*

In comparison with American or European temperate-climate gardens, showing dynamic changes from season to season, Japanese gardens remain static, varying little with the changing seasons. This contrast illustrates again differences in Eastern and Western views of life. Buddhists, certainly, tend to take the long view of the world and life—the revolving wheel that comes back to its original position—while in the West it is action, change, and pragmatic views which shape our lives. We spend little time contemplating in the sort of atmosphere where life seems to be holding its breath.

Since the Japanese garden generally is built on a small piece of land and because of its close and intimate relationship to the house and the people who live there, it has to be slowed down. Such intimate gardens which changed swiftly with the seasons would disturb and jangle the nerves of the people who came into close daily contact with them.

There are also horticultural reasons for the wide use of evergreens. Although Japan lies in the north temperate zone, its winters, tempered by warm ocean currents, are milder over most of the country than the winters of much of Europe and North America. Consequently, the frost-sensitive broadleaf varieties of evergreens survive Japanese winters. Perhaps, if American and European winters were milder, ever-greens would also assume greater importance in the basic structure of gardens in the West.

We in the West, whose homes are in areas of extreme seasonal changes, have learned to appreciate the dynamic development of a plant's life cycle. We feel something sad or beautiful and inspiring in the bare starkness of a winter landscape, and something exciting and joyous in trees bursting with spring buds. The aspects of the landscape as it shifts with each season remind us of the pulsing, rushing rhythm of our own lives. It is possible, of course, to take the middle road by striking a balance between static and dynamic effects. The final decision remains with those who will use the garden—their tastes and pace of life.

Yin & Yang. Familiarity with only the material elements of a Japanese garden, however, brings understanding up to a point which is still not at the heart of this unique art form. There are broader questions. Why is it that Japanese gardens seem to have more structural solidity and depth than most gardens in the West, gardens which by comparison seem frail, shallow, insubstantial, and meaningless? A partial answer to this question may be found in the collection of Taoist teachings, *Tao-te-ching*, formulated by Lao-tse in China several thousand years ago. This propounds the principle of opposites: in weakness there is strength; in passivity and non-resistance you win. It is the balance of light and dark, the positive *yosei* and the negative *insei*, the Yin and the Yang.

When these opposite concepts are observed in nature we find not opposition but union. One com-

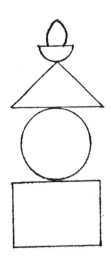

Fig. 2. These are the shapes which formed the *gorin-no-to,* or sacred stone tower, from which both the five-storied pagoda and the stone lantern were to develop. The five parts symbolize the five elements of the universe in ancient Japanese cosmology—sky, wind, fire, water, and earth. A simplified version symbolizes spirituality, consisting of heaven (the triangle) and earth (the rectangle), with man (the circle) between them.

plements the other to compose reality, the truth of creation. Japanese gardens, with their rock and plant life, embody this reality and therefore seem alive, vibrant, part of life. The positive, male element is plant life in all its forms and species. The negative, female part is the rock element in myriad shapes and sizes. Rock, decomposing and being pulverized into soil becomes the mother earth. And earth, through countless ages, is pressed again into rock—a never-ending process of decomposition and composition.

Although as compared with plant life, rock and earth would seem the stronger and more substantial, its life is of an inner quality and strength, a typical female characteristic. Trees and shrubs and grass and flowers show an active, exuberant vitality and growth. Rock and soil embody the waiting, receiving element, while plants show their impatience, spurting ahead, reaching out, externally vital.

Is it because Yin and Yang meet in a Japanese garden that it seems settled, more complete, rounded out, more stabile and solid? The two opposites are balanced so that neither one is in excess; just so does nature automatically achieve its own balance if left to itself without the interference of men. The Japanese garden artist seeks to discover this balance and to make his garden freely in whatever design or style he chooses, with rock and plant life happily wed in his composition. *(See Plates 14, 37, and 56.)*

Garden builders in the West must also assume this task if they desire to make gardens in this spirit. They may achieve this result through pure intuition. But they are more likely to be successful if they follow the example of their Japanese brothers, who, from childhood, and from the advantages of an ancient and noble tradition, have studied nature in all its forms and moods. The modern garden builder can learn more from a walk in the woods, fields, and mountains than from all the home and garden magazines and manuals. Interest, love of nature, patience, open eyes, and curiosity are the only tools he needs. For more than a thousand years of Japanese gardens this has been the lesson taught by Buddhist priest, artist, tea master, and garden designer.

Something of Symbolism. Working with rock, gravelly sand, plant material, and ceramic, stone, metal, and wooden artifacts, Japanese garden builders from earliest times have made use of certain conventional forms which have represented to them both artistic truths as well as symbols in Buddhism and Shintoism *(see Plates 7–9).* The triangle, circle, and rectangle have been considered the fundamental shapes in all design as well as geometric abstractions symbolizing the basic elements composing the universe. The triangle represents heaven or fire; the circle, water; and the rectangle, the earth *(see Fig. 2).* In a religious context the triangle symbolizes the hands of man, pressed together, pointing heavenward in prayer; the circle represents man or the mirror, one of the three most sacred Shinto symbols. To these three basic forms are added the half circle or the half moon, an abstraction denoting the wind; and a persimmon-shaped, bulbous globe for the sky. These five forms are the parts of the Japanese stone lantern.

To discover in a garden the rectangle, triangle, and circle we must think in abstract terms. One day I went with my teacher to see the famous rock, moss, and sand garden of Ryoan-ji in Kyoto *(Plate 10)*.

I reasoned that the rectangle was the outline of the garden itself, the area of sand enclosed by a low, earthen plaster wall. I then saw that a series of triangles were suggested by imaginary lines one might draw between the rocks within each group and between the rock groups themselves. But I searched in vain for the circle. Finally I turned to my teacher. "Where is the circle?" I asked. My teacher smiled and said: "Stay here for a few hours. Relax. Quietly look at the garden and you will soon become a part of it. The circle is you."

4. Conventional Classifications

SCHOLARS of the Japanese garden—in contra-distinction to those who actually design and build the gardens—have been inclined to an academic, conventional formalism in their analyses. They say that a garden must fit into a certain category and classification in order to be a valid work of art. The result has been that those who build gardens, both in Japan as well as abroad, have tended rigidly to follow rules laid down by the writers and classifiers. They have ended up copying the outer form of the garden without penetrating to the heart of the matter. This slavish copying of forms classified by scholars may be the result of the awe and respect shown in the Orient to the teacher and scholar. But it is an unquestioning subservience without any real analysis or criticism on the part of the artisan and pupil.

The classification of gardens into types and the enunciation and compilation of conventional rules came in the later years of the feudal Edo period. Previous to that time there was much greater freedom and flexibility in garden making. The garden artist-builder designed according to his own artistic judgment, without caring whether the finished product would or would not fit into any particular category. This is how it should always be. The over-conventionalization and standardization of garden design led in later years to a stultification and discouragement of originality of design. The modern garden builder, with an eye to the needs of the people who will use the garden, certainly will not want to be tied down to outworn rules and patterns. He can build his garden and achieve that wonderful unity with nature without being hemmed in by the academic restrictions of garden scholars who have done a painstaking job in classifying gardens, but have never wrestled with the problem of creating one.

The pitfalls of blindly following standard conventional patterns and rigid classifications are unmistakable. Yet for the purpose of orientation, we may benefit by knowing what these standard conventions and classifications are.

Artificial-Hill Garden. Japanese gardens have been classified into three main types. The first is the *Tsuki-yama* or Artificial-Hill Garden, which, as the name implies, contains a hill, a group of two or three hills, or a range of hills in the form of a mountain ridge *(see Plates 54 and 62)*. These elevations are then usually combined with a water feature, such as a pond or stream. Looking at the garden from the house, the hills are usually in the background, while the pond and stream are in the foreground. Often the pond has a rocky island in it, planted with grass and low shrubs, and at least one picturesquely bent pine tree. The island, originating in ancient Chinese tradition and lore, is called Horai-jima, Isle of Paradise. Sometimes there are two islands, one with a tall pine and the other with lower plantings; they represent a crane and a turtle—mythical Chinese symbols for luck and long life.

A path of steppingstones, *tobi-ishi*, winding through the garden, allows the spectator to stroll along, stopping at those spots which afford from a particular angle the most picturesque views of the garden. The garden is planted with needle and broadleaf evergreen shrubs and trees, so that it appears flourishing and alive throughout the year. They are combined with occasional plantings of deciduous trees, shrubs, and herbaceous species, which provide either blossoms or colorful foliage at different seasons. The ground-cover may be, wholly or partially, moss, lawn grass, white gravelly sand, low bamboo grass, or low trimmed shrubs, such as yew or azalea. Rock arrangements are combined with planting along the shoreline of the pond and the edges of the stream. A waterfall is often constructed near the left side of the garden. A pair of massive, tall stones, *takizoe-no-ishi*, stand on each side of the waterfall. Stone lanterns are placed at appropriate points to furnish light for walking in the garden at night and for special events, such as snow-viewing parties.

Flat Garden. A second type of garden, the *Hira-niwa* or Flat Garden, is laid out on a level, enclosed area, with no hills or water forms *(see Plates 11, 44, 56, and 70)*. Instead, it is generally a composition of trees and pruned shrubs and rocks, arranged to symbolize the natural scenery of mountains, valleys, or islands. The flat portion is covered with white gravelly sand, moss, or lawn, or combinations of these materials, to represent the sea or the flowing water of a river. Another name for this type of garden is *Kare-sansui*, literally Dry Landscape. Its charm depends upon the effect its abstract symbolism produces in the mind of the beholder, who then creates his own scenery in his imagination. Depending upon the formality of its design and its use, the flat garden may or may not use steppingstone paths.

These flat gardens exist in many of the Zen temple courtyards of Kyoto and vicinity. The most abstract and perhaps the most beautiful is that of Ryoan-ji, whose composition depends entirely on fifteen moss-edged stones arranged in a pleasing asymmetrical but balanced pattern, set in a sea of fine, white gravel *(Plate 10)*. The garden is enclosed by a low, tile-topped yellowish-brown mud plaster wall and by the portico and a wing of the temple itself.

Tea Garden. The third standard type of garden is the *Cha-niwa*, Tea Garden, which adjoins the teahouse of the traditional tea ceremony *(see Plates 52, 63, 64, and 71)*. The garden is generally divided into two parts. The outer part is the *soto-roji-niwa* or outer-entrance garden, through which the guest passes from the street gate to the waiting pavilion and then to the teahouse itself. It is usually a narrow garden, consisting of a series of changing views of naturalistic planting and sparse stone arrangements through which a garden path of steppingstones and inlaid stone pavement winds up to the teahouse. Kakuzo Okakura, in the *Book of Tea*, described the outer tea garden in this way: "Again the roji, the garden path which leads from the *machiai* (waiting pavilion) to the tea-room, signified the first stage of meditation—the

Color Plate 8. What gives this garden its sense of gentle ease and weightlessness? Do you feel an airy, floating quality? You are really invited to glide to the top of these steps rather than to climb them. The risers are low, and the soft, loose gravel treads are of especially broad and generous proportions. The delicate, soft gray, weathered tones of the elegant bamboo fence and the light-gray, almost off-white, of the gravel make a vigorous contrast with the rich, dark greens of the moss groundcover, the red pines, and the scarlet maple. This garden has strong definition as well as typical Japanese naturalness. (Juge-tsu-kan, Shugaku-in Imperial Villa, Kyoto.)

Color Plate 9. Granite rocks set in cement form a strong, defined system of paths and steps, appropriate for a public institution such as this temple and its garden. The flowering azaleas add a happy touch of color in June to the predominant gray tones. The neat, mounded forms of the sheared azaleas are like hills piled one above the other. (Kofuku-in, Nara.)

Color Plate 10. A mosaic of textures and soft tones is formed by dark gray, natural weathered rock, beige, cut-granite slabs, off-white gravel, gray pebbles, glossy green Japanese holly, and dull gray, old roof tiles. The tiles are set vertically on their edges into a bed of concrete. They tie in the natural rock with the geometrical pattern of the walk. (Detail of entrance garden, Toyoda residence, Juso, Osaka Prefecture.)

Color Plate 11. This small courtyard garden has never had a real stream of water running through it. But the stone bridge, the layout of rocks and mounded azaleas along the dry, gravelly course, and the mossy banks can stimulate the imagination. The beholder adds the water—an exercise in Zen. (Raiko-ji, Otsu.)

passage into self-illumination. The *roji* was intended to break connection with the outside world and to produce a fresh sensation conducive to the full enjoyment of estheticism in the tea-room itself. One who has trodden this garden path cannot fail to remember how his spirit, as he walked in the twilight of evergreens over the irregularities of the steppingstones, beneath which lay dried pine needles, and passed beside the moss-covered granite lanterns, became uplifted above ordinary thoughts. One may be in the midst of a city and yet feel as if he were in the forest, far away from the dust and din of civilization."

The inner teahouse garden, seen from the tea-room itself, is a small enclosed garden of simple and subdued quality with no imposing rock arrangements, but rather a composition of simple naturalistic planting and rock. The tea garden should contain those ineffable qualities of *sabi* and *wabi*, sought after and prized by Japanese tea masters and all those who take part in the tea ceremony. By *sabi* they mean the appearance of antiquity, age, hoariness, rusticity, natural textures, while *wabi*, a more abstract concept, describes the sense of quietness, astringency, good taste, and tranquillity produced in the precincts of a teahouse and garden. *(See Plates 35, 37, 39, 41, 43, and 44.)*

Three Moods. In addition to the foregoing three categories, gardens may also be classified under three styles, moods, or degrees of formality—*shin, gyo,* and *so,* the same words used to classify such diverse arts as calligraphy, painting, and flower arranging. *Shin* is the most formal, usually the style of the entry garden of a home. *Gyo,* the intermediate mood, is used as the transitional style of a side garden leading to the rear garden in *so* style, which is usually the most private and consequently the freest and most informal. *(See Plates 26 and 27.)*

PART TWO

The Practice:

5. Some Design Techniques

In planning a garden, the Japanese landscape artist employs esthetic as well as psychological principles in achieving his final effects. This requires not only a profound understanding of nature's forms but also of how men respond to them physiologically, intellectually, and emotionally. Thus, for example, the mere arrangement of steppingstones can cause the person walking in the garden either to walk awkwardly or naturally. The psychological reaction may thus be either pleasure or irritation. By the placing of steppingstones or steps over an embankment, or by making the path turn at a certain spot, he may cause the spectator walking there to turn or pause, to look up or down, directing his sight to a particularly interesting or attractive view. It is as if the garden builder were on the scene leading you by the hand through the garden, pointing out to you what is especially good, what is to be appreciated and felt.

When the garden is still in the planning stage, the designer tries, wherever possible, to make use of the natural, pre-existing features of the site. Thus, if a grove or stream or hill is already there, he tries to incorporate it into the whole composition. By integrating the garden more closely with the natural terrain outside of it, he achieves a more realistic feeling. But if there are no natural features worth preserving, the Japanese garden builder may then proceed to construct whatever land forms he feels are valid. He has at his disposal an infinite variety of shapes and sizes of mountains, hills, forests, bush, marsh, field, pond, lake, ocean, beach, islands, promontories, rivers, streams, valleys, waterfalls, etc. In some parts he may treat the landscape form with complete faithfulness to nature while in others he may have recourse to an idealistic, symbolic, or impressionistic technique. In such a case he leaves it partially or wholly up to the spectator to complete the landscape in his own mind.

The designer uses common sense and follows the laws of nature in expressing an idea or mood. He works through the shapes, textures, colors, proportions, lines, and arrangements of rocks and plants to put across his conceptions. If the effect of a high mountain is desired, the rocks must have perpendicular or abrupt sides and slopes, while a gentle hillock is represented by rocks or trimmed plants with rounded and gently sloping sides. The rocks are placed to accentuate their rocky nature for a high, rocky mountain, while to express the slope of a low, familiar hill, smaller rocks and stones are dispersed into the lawn or surrounding shrubbery.

The proportions are carefully figured. The space allotted to land and water (or water representation) is carefully calculated to present the most pleasing contrast between these two elements. Reflections in the water of trees, rocks, man-made objects, clouds, and sky are considered a part of the composition.

The garden designer also carefully considers the relationship between the over-all size of the garden and the scale of the principal man-made elements. An over-sized stone lantern, basin, rock arrangement,

bridge, or island in a small garden would reduce its sense of spaciousness. Or, if there is a navigable pond in the garden, a boat may be constructed in half the ordinary size, with the result that the pond looks bigger than it actually is *(see Plate 12)*.

Horizontal lines tend to give a sense of spaciousness. These may be found in the smooth surface of a body of water, a low shore-line, a stretch of sand or gravel raked into flowing lines, the long, low railing of a temple porch, or a low, gently sloping roof. Greater sense of space and vista is achieved on a rectangular plot of land if a pond or any other form is placed on a diagonal. If the diagonal element is water, the grading is built up so that the water flows away from the house toward the far side of the garden. The movement of water is purposely planned to create a feeling of greater depth and vista.

Further perspective is gained by placing large objects—rocks and plants—near the viewpoint of the spectator, just as in Japanese *sumi-e*, black-ink painting, where dark, bold strokes are put in the foreground. Tall hills appear nearer, while small, low hills look farther away.

Loraine Kuck, in her book *The Art of the Japanese Garden*, speaks of the effect of attaining greater perspective in her treatment of the esthetics of Kinkaku-ji, the Gold Pavilion in Kyoto *(see Plate 13)*: "From the pavilion the lake appears much larger than it really is, an effect achieved by bold and clever handling of the vistas and perspective. Standing in the pavilion, it is not until we consider the height of the trees on the opposite shore that we realize how close to us they really are. The principal device used to

Color Plate 12. These rocks were selected for the sculptural quality of their shapes and the beauty of their textures. The standing and resting postures of the rocks create a rhythmic flow of lines and masses and, at the same time, serve as symbols of real mountains and seascapes. They are set to give maximum reflection in the water. (Katsura Imperial Villa, Kyoto.)

Color Plates 13 & 14. How a path is to be used logically determines the kind of path to be made. Stepping-stones set in an irregular, zigzag pattern suggest informality and light traffic. It is a meandering, capricious route generally leading to intimate, secluded garden nooks—one's "secret place." In contrast, broader, regular, more direct, paved garden paths serve the practical function of leading you along the more heavily traveled paths around the garden, to the outbuildings, and back to the main gate. The variety of pavements and paths you encounter as you stroll along add interest and even excitement to the garden stroll. (Katsura Imperial Villa, Kyoto.)

obtain this effect is division of the lake into two parts, of which the inner, nearer half is filled with interesting rocks and an island to keep the eye busy, while beyond it the outer half is empty and dimly seen, suggesting vaguely illimitable distances. The division of the lake is made by means of a peninsula and a long island. Jutting out from the right shore, the peninsula turns what would be the lake's virtually oval form into an approximate heart outline. The long narrow island continues the line of the peninsula. A vista between them to the opposite shore is left open, and at its lower end, the lake opens into a wide sweep of clear water. In the distance, beyond the central island, are some lesser islands and rocky islets. They are deceptively small to enhance the perspective. The far shore of the lake has almost no stones visible on it, in strong contrast to the near shore of the central island and the peninsula, which hold many. This device too creates a feeling of greater distance, as if the other side of the lake is too far away for its details to be clearly seen."

In a garden which has no water features the sense of greater distance can be captured through the artful placement and choice of trees, shrubs, rocks, fences, and hedges. By planting larger trees and shrubs close to the house and smaller ones farther away the illusion of greater distance is created. If trees and shrubs are grouped so as to form a thicket or little grove in the foreground or middle distance, the effect is to mask the farther parts of the garden, which become only vaguely seen. When we look at the garden through a frame of tree trunks it appears farther away. This differs from the practice in other countries where shrubs and trees are banked along the edges of the property, strung out as a belt, with the tallest plants set in the rear and the shorter ones to the fore. The Japanese, on the other hand, while not forgetting the value of using plants for screening and enclosure effects at the edges of a property line, use the same devices as the artist and painter to enlarge the perspective. This, of course, is not playing tricks since they are merely resorting to naturalistic plant groupings which they have observed in the woods and mountains. *(See Plates 15, 35, 42, 43, 48, 62, and 206.)*

Other devices are also used to give a feeling of greater distance. Plants and materials of brighter shades and colors are employed near the house, while those of darker shades are put in the distance. Trees and shrubs with large leaves or with a heavy mesh of branches are planted near the house, while, at the rear, plants of finely textured leaves and branches are used. If something attractive, interesting, or unusual is placed near the house, such as a stone lantern, water basin, stone figure, or rock arrangement, the eyes are occupied with the foreground and not with the background. A curving path that winds among trees and shrubbery, now appearing, now disappearing, partially masked by thickets, looks farther away than it actually is. Or, sometimes resort is had to an optical illusion. For example, a small sand garden or a plot of lawn is laid out so that its back width is slightly narrower than its width closer to the house. The perspective of the garden thus appears to recede faster into the distance.

On the other hand, if the designer wants to foreshorten the perspective as viewed from the house, he may merely reverse the techniques described above. Or, instead of grading the garden to gently slope away from the house, he may heap up soil to form a ridge or ascending slope planted with big trees at the farthest extremity of the ridge. A hill or ridge built up in the middle ground also takes away the sense of greater distance.

The Japanese try not to show everything from any one spot. This effect creates mystery, stimulating the spectator's imagination. Each view witholds some part of itself from complete revelation. One never sees from any one point where a path leads: its course is hidden at each twist and turn by rocks, a hillock, or shrubbery.

In a small flat garden in the lower portion of Shugakuin Imperial Villa in Kyoto, there is a white, finely graveled path winding through islands of clipped, low shrubberies, rocks, and flowers. Seated on the portico of the temple adjoining the garden, you catch glimpses of the path's white surface. It is a strangely tantalizing effect. You feel the desire to get up and follow the path's meanderings. Or you can imagine it as a silvery stream winding through the woods.

The following paragraphs describe a few of the miscellaneous principles used in the design of Japanese gardens:

If the entire surface of a garden slopes precipitously and continuously either away from or toward the house, it gives a feeling of instability and foreshortens the depth of a garden. Portions of the sloping ground should be leveled off at several elevations between the house and the far edge of the garden.

If you want a mountainous feeling near the house, soil may be piled up to form a mound or hillock (see Plate 152). Rocks should then be set into the grass or vine-covered slopes so that they appear as natural rock outcroppings. Other rocks should be arranged in a naturalistic grouping concentrated about an interesting feature, such as the tang of a hill, near a tree, or as supports for one of the columns or posts supporting some architectural element of the building or other adjacent architectural feature.

Where natural drainage is poor, a slight slope should be made on the surface of the ground to carry away excess rainfall. Or drainage pits should be dug, filled with rocks, gravel, sand, or brushwood, and covered with a layer of soil. If is not possible to drain the ground using these mechanical devices, it at least helps to plant in the area large-leafed deciduous trees, whose roots take up much water and evaporate it through the leaves. Maples are especially good for this purpose. The ground should be planted with grasses and ferns which grow well in damp spots. Or cover the ground with sand or gravel.

Do not plant broad-leafed deciduous trees over needle evergreens. It is better to plant them under the evergreens, which allow some sunlight to filter through to the deciduous plants beneath.

In planting three or more shrubs or trees or in setting three or more rocks, care should be taken so that they do not lie in one line, either horizontally or in depth.

Trees and shrubbery of one species are often grouped together in mass to get an effect of strength or substance. For example, cryptomeria, hinoki

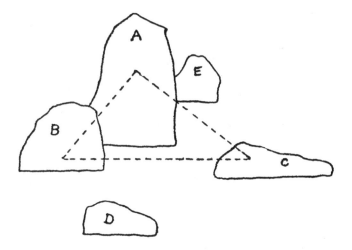

Fig. 3. Diagram of a rock composition in a non-equilateral triangle. **A,** the main or face rock, receives its lateral balance when **B** and **C,** the side rocks, are set into the ground. **D** and **E,** the smaller front and back rocks, are then added to give further stability to the arrangement. Sheared shrubs such as azaleas are planted with regard to the same principles of occult balance.

cypress, pine, bamboo, oak, or birch are often planted to form a grove or thicket. On the other hand, sometimes for the sake of attaining interesting contrast in form, texture, or color, a maple is planted among a group of evergreens.

In general, rocks, shrubs, and trees with sharp, pointing, vertical crowns convey the feeling of striving action, and struggle. On the other hand, rocks and plants with rounded shapes give a calm, settled, more restful feeling.

The leaves and branches of a plant tend to grow toward the direction of the sun's strongest rays, while the roots of the plant tend to grow in the opposite direction.

Plants and rocks form better composition if they are banked up both laterally and in depth, each element masking portions of the element adjacent to it.

In all their arts the Japanese show their devotion to asymmetry in their preference for triads, the old quantity of three, the triangle. Since the imaginary triangle in a Japanese garden composition is never equilateral, balance in a composition is always occult rather than evident. In any arrangement of hillocks, rocks, or plants, the base of the triangle (the longest side) is placed approximately parallel with the main line of the architectural element *(see Fig. 3).* For example, in a rock arrangement simulating a waterfall, the tallest stone (cascade stone) is at the apex of the triangle. The front and rear rocks are then added to give greater perspective and an impression of stability and balance.

The patina of age and antiquity is prized. The Japanese love the unpainted grain of wood, textures and surfaces that have weathered to a soft grey, rocks that are covered with lichens and moss, the tans and browns and earth colors of roof tiles, rough pottery, mud plaster, woven straw, grass, and twig fences, mats, and garden screens. Wooden fence posts or tree supports are often slightly fire-charred before they are used to remove the look of newness. The expression of *sabi* and *wabi* is most clearly seen in the choice of the most natural, unassuming, and unobtrusive colors and surfaces.

Bamboo harmonizes well with beige colors, such as are found in mud plaster walls. It does not go well with colorfully painted surfaces. It will blend, however, with white, rough textured surfaces. *(See Plates 117 and 119.)*

6. Arranging Rocks & Stones

IN PLACING rocks and stones in a Japanese garden, the approach is very different from that of making a rock garden in the West, where little attention is paid to each rock's individual character. In the West, moreover, there is neither a thought-out plan relating to the design which the rocks create nor of their relationship to the plant materials and to the architectural elements.

The rocks of a Japanese garden, however, are a strong, organic factor in the over-all design of the garden. They are never monotonous, but are grouped sculpturally to act as strong points and transitional elements between the house and garden. They express rhythm, sometimes by contrasting vertical and horizontal lines or by expressing a flow of lines. Natural rock forms are easily combined with rock, stone, concrete, and tile made in angular or round geometrical forms. *(See Fig. 4.)*

The over-all design and the role of all the components—architectural, plant, and rock—are first carefully figured out on paper before the work of construction is begun. The rocks (bought from a dealer or hauled out of their original locations) are then carefully selected, using all the artistic criteria at the command of the designer. The rocks are set into the ground with the aid of chain hoists and block and tackle hung from a stout tripod. Careful thought and consideration is given to each rock's relationship to the other rocks and garden materials. Often, the garden-maker, upon seeing the rocks actually on the site, will shift them to different positions or attitudes from those he had envisaged on the original plan. For, only after seeing the various rocks in juxtaposition can he use his artistic judgment in deciding how they should be finally set.

Rocks and plants complement each other *(see Plates 14–15)*. Rocks give composure to plants by carrying into the scene a feeling of solidity. Plants give composure to rocks, softening the lines, by concealing their bases and ground-level surfaces. A quiet feeling is achieved by setting a large flat rock or group of rocks by a perpendicular tree. Sharply jutting, craggy, pointed, perpendicular rocks are never good under any kind of tree. One rock is rarely set. But in the case where it is of good size, or if it appears as a natural rock outcropping, it is permitted.

Aucuba japonica, fig varieties, and other very large-leafed shrubs should never be planted over rocks. The rocks will sour and "die." Rocks in thickets of pine, oak, chestnut, and other needle evergreens provide an air of mountain forests.

The Japanese prefer granites, gneisses, schists, andesites, and other metamorphic rocks because of their hard texture, age, and weathered quality. Contrary to popular belief in the West, the best Japanese gardens never use rock of volcanic origin—the porous blue, black, and red hardened lava stone—as it has no character. Fortunately, almost every country of

Fig. 4. Some typical rock groupings, both asymmetrical and balanced.

the world is filled with a great variety of fine metamorphic rock, the equal of the best rocks found in Japanese gardens.

Since rocks express characteristics of the terrain from which they were originally taken, they should not be used to denote entirely different land formations in the garden. Thus, rocks of sharp, rugged form found in the mountains conform most naturally and realistically as symbolic mountains of a garden. Similarly, rounded rock and stone taken from a river bed are best used to make the course of a garden stream.

The Japanese gardener regards a rock as natural sculpture with both good, living features that should be shown and mediocre ones that are better concealed. Before setting it in his garden, he tries always to discover the rock's "living face" to be exposed above the surface of the ground. It is not only that

part showing the most interesting colorings, seams, cracks, weathering, lichens, and mosses, but also that which bears design relevance to the designer's theme and to the rest of the garden elements.

With keen, inquiring eyes the garden designer and builder has walked the countryside, observing rock and stone in their natural environments—mountain peaks, stone outcroppings, riverbeds, and rocky seacoasts. Later, in setting rock in a garden he almost intuitively knows which side to turn to view. Like an iceberg drifting in the northern seas, nine-tenths of whose bulk is under water, so in laying rock in a garden, he buries much of its bulk below the surface of the ground. When it is finally set in position it looks as if it belongs there, firmly rooted in the soil, and has been there since the beginning of time, thrusting out of the ground, showing its best face to the world.

7. Integration of House & Garden

THERE is always a correspondence in feeling and scale between a Japanese house and its garden. In this respect it is, of course, no different from the accepted standard of good landscaping practice anywhere in the world. A large Japanese dwelling requires a garden to match its size and style—such as a naturalistic stroll garden laid out on a vast scale and containing elements of outstanding splendor, enrichment, and intricacy.

Large or small, the house is closely joined to its natural environment in one balanced, unified composition. The architectural elements are led into the landscape through the artful arrangement of trees, shrubs, grass, moss, flowers, rocks, water forms, and man-made objects, all of which suggest the partnership of nature and man. The transition cannot be made abruptly. It becomes a logical, gradual, subtle, step-by-step process going in both directions, establishing a progression of feeling from pure nature to pure art and back again.

The integration of the house and garden is accomplished by matching, or often by merely suggesting in both of these areas, correspondences in shapes, colors, textures, and lines, or by using intermediary units to serve as linking factors. Line relationships may be seen in the gentle slope of a roof, its broad, overhanging eaves, or their slightly upturned ends.

These architectural lines express the feeling found in the almost horizontal sweep of the branches of a Japanese pine tree, their counterpart in nature. Parallelism of line may also be seen in the straight shoreline of a pond or lake, the line of a fence, wall, or long clipped hedge, or the straight edges of borders of granite curbs and tile walks repeating in the garden the lines and angularities of a building. *(See Plates 1, 10, 72, 129, and 229.)*

With respect to form, we may find correspondence between the garden and the house in, for example, the geometrical shapes of square-trimmed camellia bushes, oaks, or other shrubs often planted near a building. Here, both plant and architectural material are in angular, geometrical forms; but the plant, a live, dynamic object, serves as an intermediary, quasi-architectural form with a natural, living spirit.

Water too becomes a linking factor when it is led as a flowing stream or along the shoreline of a pond extending into, under or around a building. Or, by placing near a terrace or veranda a stone water basin, *chozubachi*, with appropriate plantings of fern, moss, or other low plants at the base, the water in the basin, the plantings, and the natural granite texture and color tie together at that point the garden and the house. *(See Plates 20–22, 31–33, 36, 40, 46–49, 51, 61, 62, 64, 67, 72, 74, 75, and 195.)*

8. Water Features

AN ISLAND country surrounded by oceans, a land of abundant rainfall filling its rivers, streams, lakes, and rice paddies, it is no wonder that Japan's gardens from earliest times have contained water features of all kinds, both real and simulated.

The Japanese love all aspects of water, running, still, or dropping and falling. When it is not economically feasible to make a stream or pond in a garden or even to have a stone water basin, then the presence of water may be suggested. Sometimes a dry stream bed is laid out with plants and rocks arranged along the edges of the gravelly course. Or a level area of white gravelly sand is raked into wave patterns to sugggest an ocean shoreline. Rocks, symbolizing islands, are set into the sand-covered ground.

Streams *(see Plates 79–89)*. A murmuring stream winding through a garden injects a feeling of life and movement into an otherwise quiet and passive scene. In the Heian period these streams were led under pavilions and covered passageways between buildings, closely linking the house with the garden. The principles followed in laying out the streams were based on the garden-makers' observations of nature. An eleventh-century manuscript, *Sakutei-ki,* (Memoranda on Garden Making), written by Tachibana-no-Toshitsuna, states, in part: "In making a stream in a garden, place the rocks where the water turns: then it will run smoothly. Where the water curves, it strikes against the outer banks, and so a 'turning stone' should be set in at that point. Other rocks and stones should be laid here and there as if forgotten. But if too many stones are placed along the stream, while it may appear natural when you are close by, from a distance it will seem as if they had no purpose. Moreover, an excess of rocks will make the course seem one of stone rather than of water. Thus, the water effect will be spoiled."

Naturally, the very practical reason for placing rocks at the bend of the stream was to prevent the land from being washed away. The *Sakutei-ki* also states that "the usual places to set out rocks are where the stream emerges into the courtyard, where it curves around a hillock, where it empties into a pond, and where it bends in passing around buildings." Garden builders today still follow those practical rules *(see Plate 95).*

The planting in and along a stream bed is best composed of small plants and flowers which do not grow too fast or too tall. One often sees today the low, straight spikes of the *tokusa,* or scouring rush, along garden-stream courses. The *Sakutei-ki* mentions certain wild flowers: *giboshi, ominaeshi, kikyo,* and *waremoko*—the Funkia or Blue Plantain Lily *(Hosta caerulea* or *Funkia lanceolata),* which has light-green foliage, white or lilac flowers, and grows well in the shade; the Dahurian Patrinia *(Patrinia scabiosaefolia);* the Balloon or Bellflower *(Campanula*

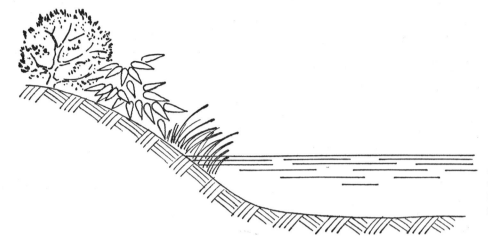

Fig. 5. Cross section of the shoreline of a garden pond or lake. At the water's edge is marsh grass; next comes sassa bamboo grass; and at the top is a low, sheared azalea.

grandiflorum), which grows in small clumps of light-green leaves with white or blue flowers about twelve inches high; and the Garden Burnet *(Poterium* or *Sanguisorba officinalis).*

The *Sakutei-ki* advises how to make a fast-running, torrent-like stream. Many rocks should be set in and along the watercourse. A rock set into a stream bed divides the flow into two rivulets whose channels should be narrowed by placing two more rocks on opposite sides of the center rock.

Where a shallow, slow-moving stream is desired, the garden hillocks should be low. Sunken rocks placed at the water's edge should be partially masked with plantings of low shrubs, grasses, and ferns, such as the low sassas and carexes. Graceful trees, like plum and willow, can also be used.

Ponds, Lakes, Islands *(see Plates 90–98).* In laying out a pond or lake, the contours of the shoreline are concealed by inlets and promontories. The shoreline is often shaped roughly in the form of the Japanese written character for heart or mind, *kokoro* 心.

In a marsh-type pond, only very few rocks are used around the edges. Waterside plants, such as *Phragmites communis, Zizania latifolia, Acorus gramineus, Iris ensata var. hortensis,* and *Iris laevigata,* are planted at the water's edge *(see Fig. 5).* Since marsh means water with little circulation, the inlet and outlet of the pond should not be readily seen. The water level should be kept high.

Various types of islands are made in garden lakes and ponds. To achieve the effect of a steep Horai-jima it should be thickly planted with evergreens. The mountains should rise one above the other, and there should be a white-sand and rock beach at the water's edge. A low, flat island suggests a moor behind a sandy beach with only reeds and grasses and moss growing among a few prominent rocks. The effect of a forested island is achieved on a low island, sparsely wooded, with low grass, sand, and a few modest rocks. A coastal cliff island is suggested by setting desolate rocks as if rising from the sea, beaten by the waves. Among these rocks there should be planted a few twisted and stunted pines. A tidal island should be partially submerged, with rocks partially seen under the surface of the water. No trees are used; only some low grasses.

In addition to rocks and planting along the banks of streams and ponds, the Japanese use fire-charred posts about three inches in diameter, which are grouped together and sunk into the soil at various heights in several places along the shoreline *(see Plates 89 and 92).* Projecting above the surface of the water, from four to ten inches, the charred posts represent old pilings and moorings.

Waterfalls *(see Plates 99–100).* Waterfalls have been classified into several types: equal quantities of water falling from two lips of the cliff, water falling off one side of the lip of the cliff, water running over irregularities on the rock face of the cliff, water made to fall away from the face of the cliff either because its top edge overhangs or because the water is supplied in great volume and force, water falling in a smooth flow over the lip like a piece of hanging cloth (caused by the smoothness and evenness of the lip of the cliff and diminished volume of water), water divided into many falling threads by numerous irregularities along the lip of the cliff, and water falling in a series of two or more cascades down step-like cliffs.

The principles of waterfall construction, found in the *Sakutei-ki* are still used today: The face of the cliff should not look artificial. The fall is usually three to four feet high. The cliff should be of mountain rock with an irregular face. Flanking rocks are set in the ground on both sides of and slightly to the front of the cliff rock. The flanking rocks must harmonize with the cliff rock. After the spaces between the cliff and the flanking rocks are filled with clay, soil mixed up with gravel is tamped in tightly between the rocks. Often a pair of rocks are set close behind the flanking rocks. Above the fall both flat and tall rocks are placed in the water and on the banks of the upper stream, as if forgotten. Rocks that slightly project forward are placed at the foot of the flanking rocks. The basin below the cascade is usually rather broad, with many rocks in the water. Further rock arrangements are carried forward downstream along the banks.

Where a natural source of water is not available for a waterfall and continually running garden stream, water pipes connected with the house water supply system are laid in the ground and led up behind the garden waterfall. If a fall or intermittent stream is not feasible, at least a thin stream of water can be made to trickle down over the face of the rock.

9. Enclosures: Fences, Walls, Hedges, Gates

SINCE the Japanese thinks of his garden and house as one indivisible space, he separates it from the outside world by fence, wall, hedge, shrub and tree screens, or artificial hills and embankments *(see Plates 101–35 and Figs. 6–53).*

The choice of materials and the design of the enclosing element—stone, wood, bamboo, mud plaster, or living plant material—are decided always on the basis of their relation to the garden and the house. They thus become integral elements of the whole composition. The enclosing element is neither obtrusive nor of such a weak nature that it could be dispensed with.

Yet garden walls, fences, hedges, and shrub and tree screens are never made so high that they completely cut off the outside world. In Japan, where land is scarce, most gardens necessarily must be made on a relatively small scale. The garden builder or homeowner, therefore, deems it desirable to gain, wherever possible, a more expansive and spacious feeling in the garden without sacrificing privacy. He may achieve this if he can look past the confines of his own garden, over his garden wall, to nearby or more distant scenery. Thus, the view of a green hill or mountainside, or a neighbor's pine tree or bamboo grove enters into and becomes a part of his own garden. When a garden is being planned, these outside views are carefully considered by the designer, who, even though he has no control over them, will make this "borrowed scenery" a real part of his design *(see Plate 2).* The Japanese have coined a word for it. They call it *shakkei.*

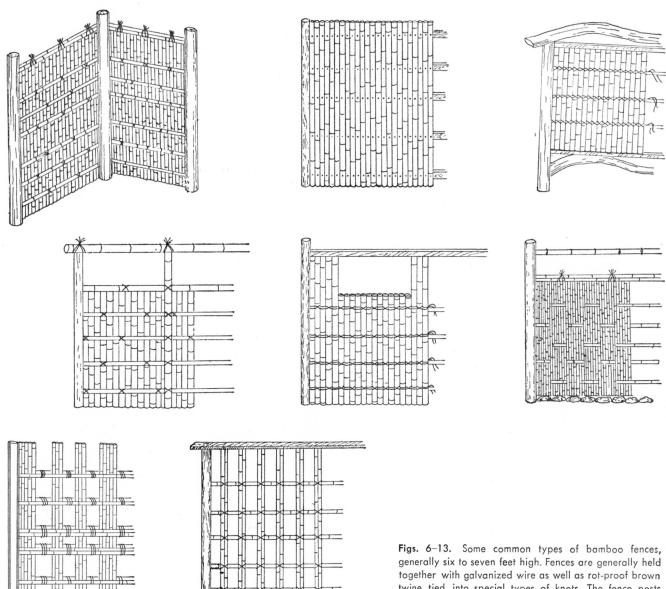

Figs. 6–13. Some common types of bamboo fences, generally six to seven feet high. Fences are generally held together with galvanized wire as well as rot-proof brown twine tied into special types of knots. The fence posts are of pine, hinoki cypress, or other sturdy timber.

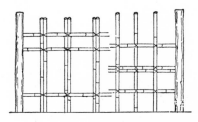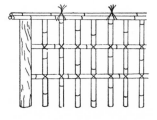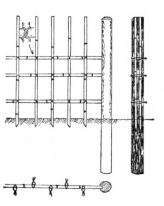

Figs. 14–16. Details of three-foot-high bamboo fences. The wooden posts are from two to three inches in diameter and are sunk sixteen inches into the ground.

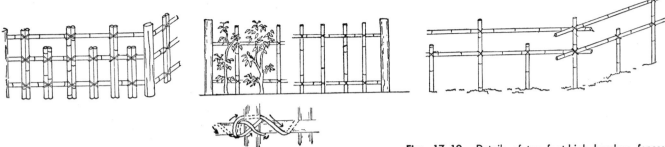

Figs. 17–19. Details of two-foot-high bamboo fences.

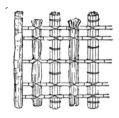

Fig. 20. A three-foot-high fence made of alternating bundles of bamboo culms and of twigs of either bamboo or shrub bush clover.

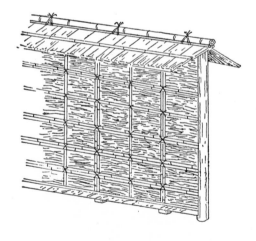

Figs. 21–22. Fences of brown-stained wood, with bamboo trim. Height is about six feet.

Fig. 23. A bamboo-trimmed seven-foot wooden fence with gabled roofing. The fence is sheathed with cedar bark.

Figs. 24–25. Fences woven from strips of cedar or cypress, with bamboo trim.

Fig. 26. Seven-foot fence of plaster and wood. The upper portion is mud plaster with bamboo-grill openings. The narrow gabled roof protects the plaster from the rain.

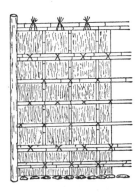

Fig. 27. Fence of cedar bark and bamboo, stabilized with wooden posts.

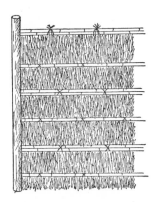

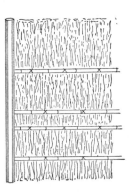

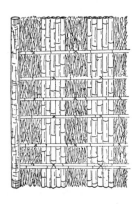

Figs. 28–30. Three fences illustrating combinations of bamboo and twigs of bamboo or of shrub bush clover. They are all stabilized by wooden posts sunk firmly in the ground.

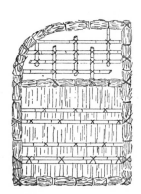

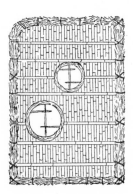

Figs. 31–37. *Sode-gaki* (sleeve fences) constructed of wood, bamboo culms, and twigs of either bamboo or shrub bush clover in various combinations and designs. They are used as garden screens and baffles adjoining the house. Generally they are from five to six feet high.

Figs. 38–49. Details of garden gates made of wood or of combinations of wood and bamboo.

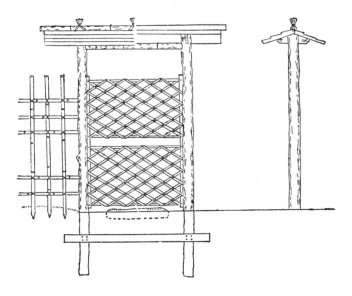

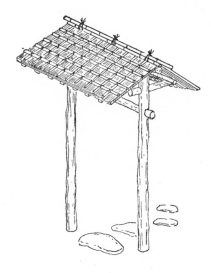

Figs. 50–52. Garden gates with gabled roofs of clapboards or cedar shingles. The upper cross-joists are about five feet from the ground. The posts are sunk two feet in the ground. The gate door shown is of split bamboo lashed to a bamboo frame with wire and twine.

Fig. 53. Garden gate made of posts with a cross-joist of the limb of a tree.

10. Steppingstones & Pavements

STEPPINGSTONES, *tobi-ishi*, and inlaid rock and cut-stone pavements, *nobedan*, carry the human touch out into the natural garden scene. They are practical, functional elements as well as integrally related parts of the composition. *(See Plates 136–71 and Figs. 54–61.)*

Steppingstones should be easy to walk on. Their tops should be reasonably flat. The distance between the stones is usually about four inches. Large stones with diameters of more than two feet are set in the middle of the center axis of the path. Smaller stones are laid along both sides of a path's center axis. Generally the axis of each stone is arranged perpendicular to the axis of the path. The height of the stones above the ground is one and a half to two inches. In tea gardens the stones are set at two to three inches above the surface of the ground. The bulk of each steppingstone is buried from five to twelve inches below the surface.

In laying a flagstone pavement it is not necessary to mortar the joints between the stones if they are thick enough to be set firmly and deeply into a hard-tamped bed of earth. Generally the space between the stones is from one quarter to one half an inch. The larger the stones, the wider the joint. In laying cut, angular stone avoid cross-type joints. They look weak.

Even if mortar is used, the joints will in time become mossy if the pavement is located in a moist, shady spot.

Steppingstones laid across water heighten interest and the feeling of adventure. They lend a touch of gentle humor and denote man's partnership with and humanization of nature. As you step from stone to stone you are brought into intimate contact with the water, causing a cool, fresh sensation, and evoking memories of childhood fantasies of adventure. They are a charming feature in any garden.

Natural rocks, cut-granite blocks, old millstones, and stone pillar footings are the usual materials, used alone or in combination. In selecting the stone the prime consideration is obtaining a flat surface which can be exposed above the water, and with enough bulk so that it can be firmly fixed in the bed of the stream. The stones are arranged in a pattern fitted to the normal human gait *(see Plates 166, 168–69, and 171)*.

Garden steps are often made by laying rock, lengths of stone curbing, or four-inch-diameter tree trunks at the rise. They are held in place by wooden stakes or rocks. Then the back is filled with tamped earth and covered with pebbles and gravel packed into the ground *(see Color Plate 1)*.

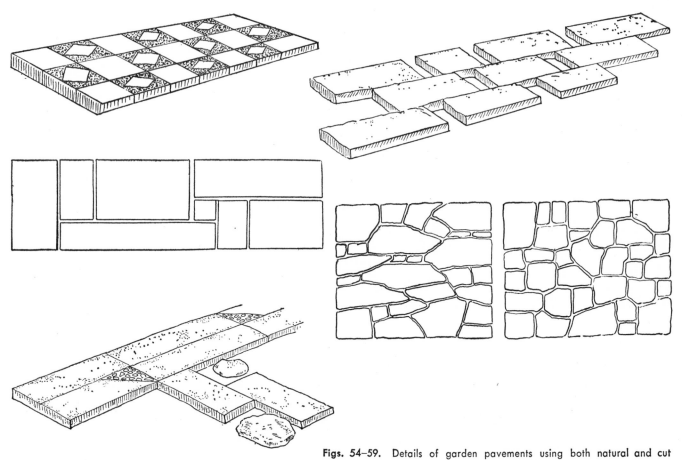

Figs. 54–59. Details of garden pavements using both natural and cut stone set in mortar matrices or having mortared joints.

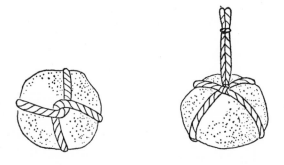

Fig. 60. *Sekimori-ishi* are used as stop signs on a garden path, indicating that one may proceed no further. The rocks are usually from three to four inches in diameter and bound in rope as shown here. (See also Plate 42.)

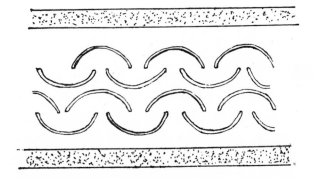

Fig. 61. Detail of granite curbing and *mune-gawara* (ridgepole tiles) set vertically into the ground. The space between may be covered either with white sand or fine, gray river pebbles. Used along a path or at the side of a building.

11. Artifacts

ARTIFACTS humanize the naturalism of a Japanese garden. They are, however, to be selected with great care and used with restraint lest they overpower the naturalism of the garden. Generally, artifacts with the simplest lines and shapes and those that show the greatest feeling of age and antiquity are preferred. They may be made of stone, ceramics, iron, bronze, or wood. They should be logically placed where, if possible, they serve some useful function—a bridge to cross a stream, lanterns to light a path, water basins that are accessible, statues and towers that can be seen from the house. Since artifacts are made of substantial materials, they are expected to endure in the garden and to become an integral part of its composition. An artifact is not to be considered as an ornamental frill, but as an object which, if removed from the garden, would take with it the integration and unity of garden, house, and man.

Lanterns *(see Plates 172–84)*. Stone, iron, and bronze lanterns are used in Japanese gardens. The metal lanterns are usually placed close to the house, set on a rock or hung from the eaves. Stone lanterns are generally placed by a water basin, along a path, or in any part of the garden where light is needed at night. Usually a rock is set from one to two feet from the base of the lantern to give it a sense of balance and stability. Snow-viewing lanterns at the edge of a pond do not need this rock. Also, if the lantern is set along a path of large steppingstones, the front rock is not needed. Sometimes the front rock may be set laterally off to one side of the lantern. If the light-housing section of the lantern is block shaped, it is better to set it obliquely to the main point of view. Three-legged snow-viewing lanterns should be set so that two legs face the main point of view. To increase the feeling of depth, lanterns may be slightly masked by plants so that at night the light is partially screened, resulting in a glimmering effect. This same effect is so highly valued in a Japanese garden that, except when practical considerations are of overriding importance, lanterns are almost never wired for electricity but are instead lighted with candles, kerosene lamps, or the like; and for the same reason the larger apertures of the light-housing section are fitted with panels of wood and translucent paper or, much less preferably, with frosted glass.

Basins *(see Plates 185–201 and Fig. 62)*. Stone water basins are a refreshing and practical link between the site and the building. They are placed with appropriate low plantings, such as ferns, either next to a veranda or porch or at strategic points along a garden path. The type used next to the veranda is called *chozubachi*. It is placed so that it can be used while standing on the veranda. *Chozubachi* may also be used farther away from the building, especially along a garden path.

Another form of the stone water basin is the *tsukubai*, which is a more intricate grouping of rock around a basin, and is used primarily in a tea-house garden as one accoutrement of the tea ceremony.

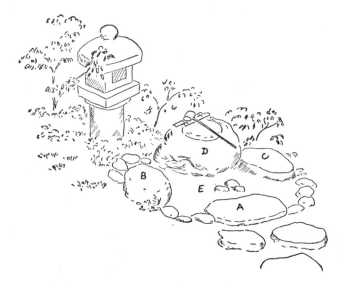

Fig. 62. A typical *tsukubai* arrangement of stone water basin, lantern, and rocks. **A** is the front steppingstone; **B** is the rock on which may be set down whatever you may happen to have in your hands at the time; **C** serves as a base for a pitcher of hot water in the winter; **D** is the basin from which water is ladled to rinse the hands; **E** is the "sea."

The water in a stone basin is furnished in several ways. It may be replenished every day by carrying water to it in a pail. It may be filled by water dripping into it from a bamboo spout set over the basin. The spout is connected to an underground pipe which is controlled from the house or by a faucet set in the ground near the basin and covered with a stone. Or, it may be furnished by piping water into the basin through a hole in its bottom. In the latter two cases, the water overflows the lip of the basin and is drained away by a covered drain set in the ground by the basin.

The *tsukubai* is made by digging a shallow recess in the ground, called the "sea," in the midst of which the stone basin is set. The walls of the "sea" are usually of a generally round or free form and built up of stones and rocks to make a shallow enclosure. They are held in place by mortar, which is applied to the rear of the rocks. Earth is pressed into the joints, and plantings of grass and ferns are naturalized in the walls of the "sea." Its floor is covered with sand or pebbles, under which lies a drainage basin. Larger rocks are grouped around the "sea" and the basin to achieve a balanced composition and also to serve the practical requirements of those who dip water from the basin to rinse their hands. There is always a front stone to stand on, a stone at the left on which to place whatever one might be holding in the hand, and on the right a rock for placing a pitcher of hot water when the *tsukubai* is used in the winter. The same arrangement is used around a well-curb,

with the stone to the right serving as a stand for the well bucket.

Sculpture, Towers, Wells. *(see Plates 202–9)*. These are most often made of granite. The sculptured figures are often of religious subjects, usually Buddhist deities. Both sculpture and towers (or pagodas) serve directly to give the garden a feeling of strong spirituality. The sculpture may be in bas-relief or in fully rounded figures, but it never is out of scale—generally up to some three feet high. Towers and sculptures are sometimes placed at the water's edge so that they form reflections in the water.

The commonest type of well-curb consists of four stone slabs fitted together to form a box-like shape, which is placed over the well. They are sometimes used in a garden as a basin for a spring, from which water brims over the top and flows away in a garden stream. In such case the water is usually artificially piped into the bottom of the well-curb, which then fills up and brims over. Today, wells have no special interest or meaning in gardens if they are not used in any way with water.

Bridges *(see Plates 210–25)*. Garden bridges always should serve the practical purpose of getting people —or the eye of the beholder—across a body of water, real or simulated. They are made of stone, wood, or wood and earth combined. The determination of the shape, size, and material of a bridge will depend upon the type of water barrier it is to traverse. Thus, a strong, bulky stone or heavy wood bridge is necessary to span a rushing torrent of water, while a delicate wood or stone bridge is appropriate for a gently trickling stream.

A stone bridge may be of one or two spans. The higher it is above the surface of the water, the more necessary it is to ensure its stability by placing large, deeply embedded bolster rocks under both ends of the span. The sense of strength and stability is enhanced by setting vertical "anchor" rocks at the ends of the bridge. The longer and thicker the span, the bigger and more imposing are the "anchor" rocks. The selection of the proper bridge and adjacent rocks depends upon the style and scale of the garden. Bridges should be set so that the sides are seen at an oblique angle from the main point of vantage, usually the veranda or terrace of the house *(see Plate 219)*.

Sand Designs *(see Plates 226–33)*. The so-called rock and sand gardens of Japan are simple abstractions of nature. They are usually made in relatively small, flat spaces enclosed by fences, walls, or hedges. Strictly speaking, the groundcover is not really sand but a decomposed (rotted) natural granitic gravel, of a whitish or light gray color, often with tiny black or reddish specks mixed in. When spread out, the material has a soft, off-white tone. The grains range in size from one-sixteenth to three-eighths of an inch. Deposits of the gravel are generally found at the foot of cliffs composed of the same soft, frangible, granitic rock. Through the process of weathering and erosion, the grains of the rock loosen and crumble,

dropping off the face of the cliff onto a talus slope below, where deep deposits eventually accumulate. These deposits are dug and the material sold for garden groundcover. In Japan these deposits are found mostly around Kyoto, especially in the Shirakawa section of Higashi-yama.

The designs raked into the sand by a wood-toothed rake generally symbolize aspects of still or flowing water. They may be mere parallel lines, straight or wavy undulations, symbolizing water in a stream or breaking along a shoreline. Or the design may be a series of concentric circles representing raindrops falling into a pool, making ever-widening circles.

The gravelly sand is usually laid two to three inches thick over hard-tamped earth. Since these areas are not walked upon, they hold the design for a number of days. After a storm or heavy rain the lines are re-raked into the surface. It is necessary to add a fresh layer of sand periodically. *(See Plates 53–55 and 78–80.)*

Sound Effects *(see Plate 234)*. Besides pleasing visual effects, the Japanese garden builder does not overlook the effect of garden sounds made by wind, water, or insects. A grove of bamboo or pine trees are often placed so that they catch the wind. The sound of wind or wind-driven rain swishing and rushing through bamboo is one of the memorable pleasures in a Japanese garden.

The sound of water is another important element. It may be the splash of water falling from a cascade, the gurgle of a brook as it rushes over its rocky, gravelly course, or the faint tinkle of drops of water

Color Plate 15. November brings the fire of scarlet and crimson maple leaves into a Japanese garden. The bright colors are a fleeting but exciting change. By December the evergreens regain their sway, ruling once more in their static kingdom. (Katsura Imperial Villa, Kyoto.)

Color Plate 16. Each rock in this garden facing a temple porch was selected with special attention to its pleasing texture and shape. The sheared azaleas and hollies are shaped into regular, mounded forms but are planted in the irregular patterns of nature. The pond acts as a buffer as well as a link between the cultivated areas close to the buildings and the more unrestrained, naturalistic plantings on the far side of the water. (Sambo-in, Daigo, Kyoto Prefecture.)

Color Plate 17. Topiary makes sense when used, not as a frill or decorative appendage, but rather as a tectonic element of the garden structure. The sheared broadleaf evergreen shrubs in cube and globular forms become integral, organic parts of the composition. They bring a sense of order to the busy, meandering pattern of the paths and a strong, three-dimensional feeling to the otherwise flat plane of the ground. (Katsura Imperial Villa, Kyoto.)

trickling from a bamboo spout into a stone basin or pool.

The whirring, chirping sounds of insects bring a warm and friendly atmosphere into Japanese homes. In the summer and fall the singing crickets in tiny cages swinging from the eaves serve as one more binding and integrating factor between man and nature.

The Japanese love to strike wood upon wood to create a hollow, haunting noise. Even today in Japanese cities and towns fire watchmen walk through the dark streets at night rhythmically hitting two sticks of wood together as they make their nocturnal patrols. The sharp, hollow, clacking noise signifies to the people in their homes that all is well.

Indeed, the striking of these sounds has a relationship to Zen philosophy. A story is told of a monk who in ancient times was cutting weeds one day in the garden of a ruined temple. A piece of tile he cast aside struck against a bamboo. At that instant he was enlightened. Sokei-an, the Zen priest who told this story, went on to question the reader in this way: "Do you think perhaps you will be enlightened if you strike a chair with your broom handle while you are sweeping the kitchen floor? You must not forget the quietude of the silent vale between the mountains where the monk had been meditating day and night alone. When the stillness of the valley was rent by the sharp crackle of the tile, in that moment he awakened to his intrinsic wisdom."

12. Garden Care & Plant Pruning

A well-kept Japanese garden, despite its naturalism and asymmetry, has an orderly and well-groomed appearance. Weeds, dead leaves, and old blossoms are removed. Garden paths are cleaned with twig brooms and bamboo rakes. Trees and shrubs are pruned regularly to keep the proper balance and proportion between the elements of the composition. The gardener tries to find the happy medium between foliage and branches growing in wild disorder without meaning and those pruned to the point where man's dominance is too patently evident. *(See Plates 235–39 and Figs. 63–70.)*

They have learned that it is wrong to bury a house in an overwhelming mass of plant material so that it loses its own personality. They recognize that the people who have to live in such a place will also feel smothered by uncontrolled planting. The lines of a building, on the contrary, are only to be complemented by the planting around it, each serving as a foil for the other.

The plants in a Japanese garden require regular pruning, clipping, shearing, pinching, or plucking. By discovering the hidden artistic potentialities in a plant the Japanese gardener can emphasize these qualities, eliminate distracting elements, simplify its lines, and thus reveal its true nature to the world. Thus a tree or shrub, in a sense, becomes an abstraction. Though its form may be naturalistic, it may also symbolize larger or grander elements of the natural landscape. Plants trimmed in geometrical shapes—round or angular—as well as man-made objects serve as foils of the naturalistic forms in the composition. The branch of a plum tree or Japanese holly, for example, trailing in front of a stone garden pagoda or stone lantern gives a softening effect. In the same way, plants trimmed into geometrical forms, when placed in the foreground or background of elements of naturalistic form, such as rocks or maple trees, give some feeling of order and security to what otherwise might be a rather lonely or wild scene. The concept of control of growing elements is vital in a Japanese garden. It is not one of man's mastery of nature, but rather of his alliance and cooperation with nature, in which man serves only as its instrument.

The characteristic spreading shape of a pine tree in a Japanese garden, with its long, low, lateral branches extending far out from the trunk, is the result of yearly pruning started in its early growth. Close examination of the tree's limbs reveals that although each one follows a generally straight course extending away from the trunk, it actually is a series of slight twists and turns which keep the branch growing on a single course. The purpose of this type of pruning is to allow the sunlight to penetrate down even to the lowest limb of the tree, remaining vigorous after many years of growth. The Japanese feel that a low, spreading shape is the most beautiful and most expressive of the pine's personality *(see Fig. 44)*.

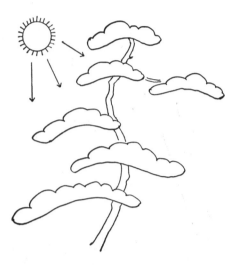

Fig. 63. A stylization of the ideal elemental form of a pine which has been pruned for early growth. Cutting out of excess branches opens up the tree, permitting the sun's rays to filter down to the foliage of the lower limbs.

Aside from artistic reasons and the necessity to control excessive growth and spread, plants are pruned and trimmed for purely horticultural purposes. Pruning may be done to rejuvenate a plant by cutting it down to the stump, thereby stimulating the growth of healthy new shoots. This is especially practiced with willows, birches, laurels, rhododendrons, and privets. Rejuvenation may also be accomplished by cutting out of suckers and parallel branches. This leaves more nourishment for the other branches. And, of course, pruning must be done at any time to remove dead or diseased parts of a tree or shrub.

In general, less drastic pruning and trimming of trees and shrubs is advisable in areas of unfavorable growing conditions, such as poor soil (sandy, dry, or hard-packed clay), polluted air (smoke, chemical fumes, or motor-vehicle exhaust), and the briny salt air at the seashore.

The time for pruning depends upon the type of plant and on whether it blooms on the previous year's wood or on that of the current year. Evergreens should be clipped, pinched and plucked in May and again in September. Some sappy maples, birch, and dogwood bleed when pruned in March and April when the sap is still in its upward course. Such plants should be pruned in the fall. Pinching off or clipping back the tips of twigs and small branches can be done at any time of the year. Thinning out the upper branches

of fruit trees to allow more sunlight into the lower ones is a way of stimulating fruit production. February and March are the best months for this type of pruning.

In ordinary situations, without the influence of man or adverse growing conditions, most plants have the tendency to grow straight in a perpendicular position. The Japanese feel, however, that although perpendicular forms of trees are good and should be used in a garden, there should also be trees and shrubs with bent, twisted, and curving lines. Such trees and shrubs provide a pleasing contrast with the straight forms of others. They lend an atmosphere of age to the garden. The rhythm in the lines of a curved branch seen against a background of a wall, fence, or hedge is a desirable effect.

There is nothing occult or magic about the techniques of training and controlling the shape of plants, practiced by Japanese gardeners from generation to generation. They are really simple and practical. The gardener in the West can accomplish the same results. He must first decide upon the artistic effect he wants to produce. Using his imagination, he should consider what would be a pleasing effect if the tree were in some other shape or position. This process is a dynamic one since the shape changes as the tree gets older. Smaller trees and shrubs may even be shifted, moved or turned to reveal a more pleasing effect. But the control of shape is primarily achieved

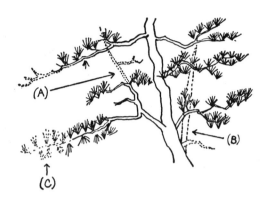

Fig. 64. Pine-tree pruning. (A) Vertical branches are cut out to stimulate the growth of lateral side branches. (B) *Zuai* pruning, the cutting out of limbs growing from the trunk vertically or in general not parallel to the rest of the limbs. (C) Trimming the tips of branches when necessary to allow more sun to penetrate to the inside areas of the tree.

Fig. 65. *Sashide*. The branches and twigs projecting below the limb are pruned off to achieve a feathery, wing-like effect.

Fig. 66. A stylized detail of *kuruma-zukashi* pruning, used especially on camellias and *Podocarpus macrophylla*. Observed from above, the effect is that of a series of cart wheels, the limbs being the spokes, and the trunk, the hub. The limbs are pruned so that none is directly above another. This permits sunlight to penetrate the entire tree, keeping the lower branches healthy.

by judicious pruning. For example, if a gardener feels that a particular straight branch is of no interest, he should cut it off just above a bud or another branch. The effect then is that the remaining lower portion becomes the main branch and receives the nourishment which formerly went mostly to the amputated part of the former main branch. The line of the limb has then, of course, been altered. Now, instead of advancing straight out, the limb turns or curves in another direction. In general, the Japanese prefer the branches of any tree to grow in an upward, curving sweep to give the effect of a wing-like plume.

Another kind of pruning is the cutting out of side, ascending, straight branches, not parallel to other more horizontal branches. These almost vertical branches are actually suckers of several years' growth which were not cut out when they first appeared. They have no value for the tree and contribute nothing artistic to its appearance.

Many Japanese like the over-all appearance of a tree to give the effect of layers of foliage laid irregularly one over the other, with light or air space in between each layer. It is almost as if the foliage were thin, feathery clouds or layers of mist. This is especially liked in Kyoto, whose surrounding mountains and mists provide the inspiration for this most charming effect, which is called *sashide*. This technique is mainly one of cutting out the main tips of branches and also pruning off the small branchlets which project downward. Thus an upward, sweeping, and tufty effect is achieved. This is especially appreciated with varieties of arborvitae, hemlock, black and red pine, maples, bamboos, and podocarpus.

Kuruma-zukashi is one more type of pruning, in which the tree or shrub is shaped so that it appears to be a series of wheels or disks laid one on top of the other with air space between each layer. The branches appear to be like the stylized clouds of Japa-

Fig. 67. New buds on the twigs of a pine tree in April and May, sprouting from the wood of the previous year's growth. The area within the dotted line is enlarged in the following figure.

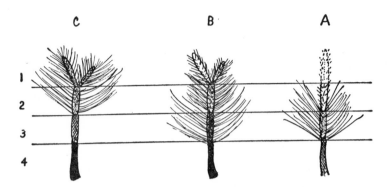

Fig. 68. The three stages of annual care of a pine tree's new buds, twigs, and needles. (An enlargement of the bud and twig within the dotted lines of the preceding figure.)

(A) The pine bud and twig as it appears in April and May. (B) The same twig in July. (C) The third stage of development in September and October.

(1 & 2) This spring's growth up to April-May. (3) Last year's growth. (4) The growth of the year before last.

In April-May two-thirds of each new bud must be pinched off as seen in A–l. By July, one, two, or three new buds have sprouted from the pinched-off stub of the new bud, as seen in B–1 and B–2. In September–October the needles growing on last year's wood are plucked off, as in C–3. Also, some of the needles growing on this year's C–2 are plucked to thin out the growth.

If three new buds have sprouted from the pinched-off stub, the middle bud is cut off in the fall. The following year the longer of the twin buds may also be cut off for the purpose of retarding the tree's growth and thinning out the foliage, so that more sunlight can penetrate.

nese classical painting which served to separate various scenes. *Kuruma-zukashi* is used on podocarpus, hemlock, camellia, sazanka, and others, especially where they are part of more formal compositions, such as the entranceway or front garden of a house, temple, or teahouse. *(See Plate 237.)*

The characteristic floating, wing-like feeling of the branches and foliage of Japanese pine trees is the result of a special way of pinching and plucking that is done twice a year. In April and May the tip of the young, tender bud at the end of each twig is pinched off, using the fingernails of thumb and forefinger, leaving about one inch of the bud at the end of each twig. This treatment controls the spread of the branch. From the remaining part of the young bud fine, dense needles will sprout during the spring and summer growing season. Again in September a second trimming is performed. This time the needles which have sprouted below the bud along the twig of the previous year's growth are plucked off with the fingers. This treatment gives the tree a light, airy, floating feeling.

The Japanese give special winter protection to the less hardy plants, such as the cycas palm and certain evergreens which are most easily victims of snow, ice, sleet, and bitter cold. This is especially true in the mountain regions and in the north. Unlike deciduous trees, evergreens are hard hit by snowstorms because of the large surfaces offered by their needles and leaves. If they do not receive some form of protection, they are frequently badly deformed, twisted, and broken by heavy snows and ice. Such plants as the yews, junipers, arborvitae, retinosporas, hollies, rhododendrons, azaleas, and others, especially those with pendulant twigs and branches, receive, where needed, special winter wrapping.

Coarse-woven rice straw matting is wrapped around the plant and tied with rice straw twine. The tops of the plants are capped with pointed bonnets made of

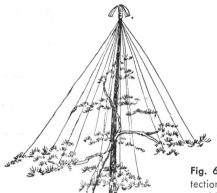

Fig. 69. A pine tree rigged for winter protection against wet, clinging snows, which would bend and break its lateral branches. From the top of the pole strings run out to all the vulnerable branches.

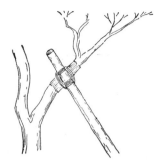

Fig. 70. The pole is set into the ground and lashed to the limb of a tree which needs support. The pole is charred or stained to blend with the dark bark of the tree.

the same material. In America, burlapping may be substituted for the straw matting but it has not the same pleasing effect. An entirely different method of protection may be employed on young, low pine trees in areas where the danger is not so much from killing, cold temperatures as from heavy, wet, clinging snows and ice. A stout pole projecting above the highest branch of the tree or shrub is sunk into the ground near the base of the trunk. Then, lengths of cord or rope are attached to the top of the pole. Each length of cord is then tied to a branch of the tree as if it were supporting the branch. The finished treatment looks like a maypole with streamers hanging down from the top, each one tied to a different branch. In heavy snows the branches are held up by the lines attached to the top of the pole.

To protect moss, which is sensitive to extreme cold, the Japanese cover it in the winter with a layer of dry pine needles, achieving a practical end as well as a pleasing effect in itself.

PART THREE

The Realization:

IF THE photographs that follow inspire new attitudes and fresh approaches to garden design, and if, as I believe, they provide material for study and inspiration beyond anything words could ever provide, then this book will have served a good purpose.

Is it not possible to work toward goals of refinement and vigor in landscaping through abstraction rather than conventionalization of forms that are peculiarly Japanese? This should not be merely for the sake of modernity, but rather to uncover in order to analyze basic artistic structure. With full freedom and an open mind, the modern, creative garden-maker in Japan moves along such paths, combining the best of the past with design to fit the present. Here, in these photographs, are his results, for us to use as we will, slavishly or creatively.

These gardens are, in some cases, not the products of professional landscape designers, but were laid out by architects, painters, writers, Buddhist priests, antiquarians, movie directors, physicians, potters, and tea masters—men separated in time and working alone. Yet they all shared a love of nature, refinement of taste, and, with wondrous economy of means, the ability to organize space.

Perhaps a word should be said concerning the order of the plates. Any one photograph can often illustrate so many different points in the text—and points far beyond anything any text could say—that any arrangement was certain to be contradictory and overlapping. Hence it has seemed best to attempt nothing too rigid, but instead, as indicated by the occasional headings to the following pages, merely to group the photographs roughly in the order of the preceding chapters. This purely arbitrary arrangement has then been made more flexible by numerous cross references between text and photographs throughout the book. As an exception to this order of the plates along the lines of the preceding chapters, a large number of miscellaneous and highly important photographs, Plates 16–78, though they might be considered as illustrations to Chapter 7, Integration of House and Garden, have actually been grouped according to the three viewpoints of the beholder: Entrance Garden, Looking from House to Garden, and Looking from Garden to House. These are the three big categories of the problem of garden design which every garden-maker must face, and this arrangement seemed the most functional.

In looking at Japanese gardens, though your eyes are on the outward forms, keep your mind upon the spirit that generated them. Do not be led astray by bizarrerie and violent asymmetry, by the strangeness of tree trunks in their natural condition built into teahouses, nor by *sabi*, the love of the atmosphere of age. For the really enduring and universal attraction of Japanese garden design is its idealized conception of artistic clarity, simplicity, cheerfulness, warmth, and faithfulness to the materials of nature. And this, then, is just where the story begins. . . .

The Theory

(Plates 1–11; see text pages 3–21)

Plate 1. Water, bubbling up out of the stone well-curb, flows over the lip and streams into a pebble-and-rock watercourse laid out several feet away from the gray-tile terrace. Yew, sassa bamboo grass, ferns, and moss groundcover produce a pleasant woodland feeling. Steppingstones lead from the terrace, cross the stream, and enter the bamboo gate. (Minoko, Kyoto.)

Plate 2. The contrast of a controlled garden set against a background of pure nature. The distant mountain view enters into the composition and becomes an integral part of the garden. Pines, maples, oaks, and evergreen shrubs compose the basic plant materials. Broad, trimmed hedges, containing a variety of evergreen and deciduous shrubs of different textures and color, and the clean shoreline of the lake serve to retain a cultivated, controlled, secure feeling in the garden despite its lush background. (Shugaku-in Imperial Villa, Kyoto.)

Plate 3. What gives this simple backyard garden its lasting charm? The groundcover is moss, gray river pebbles, and steppingstones leading to a bamboo gate at the right. The 1300-year-old Buddhist stone sculpture infuses strength of substance and spirit into the garden; its mossy, lichen-covered solid body contrasts with the more delicate textures and shapes of the other elements. The long, low clump on the left is sassa bamboo grass. The taller plantings are camellia and a young maple. Clumps of ferns, bushy grass, and low coral ardisia (*Ardisia crispa*) with its red berries dot the ground. The wall at the left is covered with hinoki-cypress bark. Persimmon trees behind the fence, seen against the stark white walls of the storehouse, create both continuity and contrast. (Aihara residence, Fushimi, Kyoto.)

Plate 4. A stroll garden, filled with a variety of embellishments. As you walk, your eyes encounter a series of changing views and effects that are gems of elegant simplicity. But, taken as a whole, the garden of this villa produces esthetic indigestion. There is just too much in the garden. It is too rich fare for the ordinary man to be able to digest and appreciate. Yet you can learn much from it. Where the architectural theme is predominant, the rock element is less in evidence, playing a secondary role. Where the growing plant component is in mass, however, rocks are dominant to balance out the weight of the trees and shrubs. (Shokintei Tea Pavilion, Katsura Imperial Villa, Kyoto.)

Plate 5. A garden of clipped azaleas and Japanese red pine. Planted on slightly different levels, the sheared forms of the azalea give the sculptural feeling of rock. White, gravelly sand paths, like valley streams, wind through the shrubbery. (Doi Inn, Kyoto.)

Plate 6. The straight, horizontal lines of the clipped six-foot hedge of mixed evergreens and the wooden fence and gate form a pleasing contrast with the tall pines and the picturesque low Japanese maples. It is as if the motive of the designer was to bring you immediately into a relatively uncontrolled, naturalistic landscape, where nature, at first sight, seems to have the upper hand. (Shugakuin Imperial Villa, Kyoto.)

Plates 7-9. The *giboshi* finial, used on posts and columns of temples and bridges of Kyoto, is a stylized form of the lotus flower, a Buddhist symbol. (Nishi Hongan-ji and Sanjo Bridge, Kyoto.)

Plate 10. Ryoan-ji, Kyoto. ▶

Plate 11. The small, interior *kare-sansui* garden of a Zen temple. This is said to have been inspired by old Chinese monochrome landscape paintings of the Sung dynasty. The symbolism of a natural mountain landscape is perhaps too obvious. The rocks, moss, and gravelly sand combine to form a sculptural composition that is striking though also contrived in feeling. The sand is raked into a pattern of flowing water. The back plantings are camellia and Japanese white pine (*Pinus parviflora*). (Daisen-in, Daitoku-ji, Kyoto.)

Plate 12. A lake in a 500-year-old moss garden. The trees and shrubs growing along the irregularly jutting and indented shoreline create a series of planes that enhance the perspective and feeling of mystery as they retreat into the distance. (Saiho-ji, Kyoto.)

Plate 13. Kinkaku-ji, Kyoto.

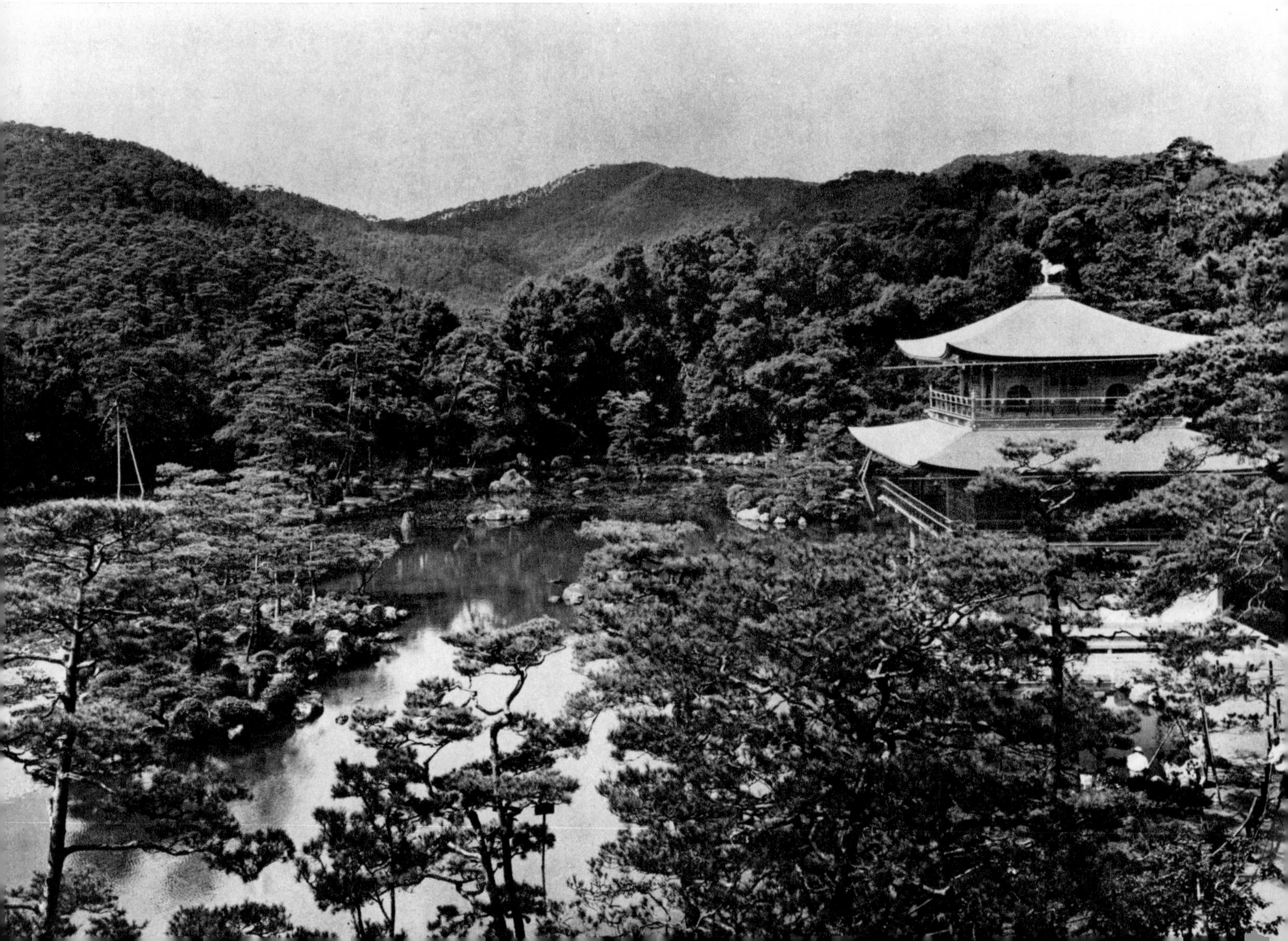

Plate 14. Nandina combined with a rock grouping in a moss groundcover. The mud-plaster wall is a warm beige color. (Tomita Villa, Kyoto.)

Plate 15. An arrangement of rocks with evergreen oak and azalea, dominated by the *Ternstroemia japonica* tree at the far corner of this temple garden. The flat rocks in the middle ground, projecting out of the sand surface, give the scene more depth and balance. (Hojo, Daitoku-ji, Kyoto.)

The Entrance Garden

(Plates 16–34; see text pages 51–52)

Plate 16. A step through the gate brings you into a suddenly transformed atmosphere that is light, gay, and whimsical. A bubbling brook skips down over a series of mossy rock ledges from its rocky source under a clump of bamboo. The stream bed, cutting across the flagstone path at the foot of the rock steps, flows beneath you as you ascend the garden steps to the front door. The bamboo-covered walls of the house link up with the bamboo growing in the garden. Other plantings of Japanese red pine, maple, plum, sassa bamboo grass, ferns, and other grasses, though completely under control, make this front garden into a pleasant, sunny woodland glade. The water source is supplied from the house water main and is controlled by a faucet concealed under a small rock. (Akaza residence, Uchinada, Ishikawa Prefecture.)

Plate 17. The narrow, front entranceway of a house set far back from the street and closely surrounded on all sides by neighboring buildings. A high wooden gate separates the garden from the street. The pavement is a variegated pattern of cut gray granite about four inches deep, set in a shallow concrete bed. The walls are covered with hinoki-cypress bark. Above eye level the bare wood has weathered to a soft gray. The low shrubbery on both sides of the path is azalea and camellia. The tree in the right foreground is Japanese pittisporum. Interspersed between the low plantings on the left are clumps of bamboo. Moss covers the ground underneath the shrubbery.

Plate 18. The delicacy and handling of the materials in the entranceway of this 200-year-old house remind you of a Japanese flower arrangement. Against the light beige of the earthen-plaster wall and the darker brown of the bamboo siding, the accents of tall nandina, low daisies, and the sparse, graceful branches of the maple stand out in pleasing contrast. The sculptured stone column gives strength to the composition. In the nearer foreground (not in the picture) water drips from a bamboo spout into a low stone water basin surrounded by a few fern fronds. The ground-cover is the stone pavement and river pebbles. (Aihara residence, Fushimi, Kyoto.)

Plate 19. The water in the basin and the clump of bamboo add ▶ both gentleness and vitality to the design of this entranceway to a private home. The stone lantern gives a warm, yellow light. (Kyoto.)

Plate 20. The pebble-covered entranceway has a clean, cool feeling. The bamboo subtly contains the pebbles within the bounds of the structure, yet they find a correspondence with the larger stones outside. (Omote Senke, Kyoto.)

Plate 21. A teahouse garden with pavement of natural rocks and cut granite set in a concrete bed about four inches deep above a three-inch layer of sand. The planting consists of Japanese red pine, evergreen oak, camellia, and *Ternstroemia japonica*. The moss groundcover ties in with the moss covered roof. (Ichi-riki, Kyoto.)

Plate 22. A temple entranceway garden. The vertical lines of the five *Podocarpus macrophylla* trees correspond to the vertical lines of the wood panelling. The azalea hedge and the stone pavement carry into the garden the horizontal lines of the gate and roof. (Myoshin-ji, Kyoto.)

Plate 23. This front entrance garden of a Zen temple has austere simplicity, in black, white, and gray. The curving lines raked in the sand repeat the curves of the roof. The plant materials, however—shrubby yew podocarpus, *Ternstroemia japonica*, Japanese black pine, and plum—infuse a subtle softness and warmth. (Kennin-ji, Kyoto.)

Plate 24.   The front entranceway of a teahouse restaurant. A quiet, clean atmosphere greets guests here as they leave the noise and traffic of the street. On the right is a mossy bed in which are planted two *Podocarpus macrophylla* trees, sassa bamboo grass, and *Ardisia japonica*. The clump of bamboo on the left blends into the split-bamboo wall. The sliding glass doors, frosted down two-thirds of their length to give privacy to entering and departing guests, convey a soft, cloud effect. The flagstone pavement is constantly kept moist to retain a fresh, cool, inviting feeling. The lamp fixture is a stylization of an old Japanese andon. (Sassakawa, Tokyo.)

Plate 25. The Sassakawa presents from the outside a simple, harmonious composition. The fence is stained a flat black. The plants projecting over the fence add a dynamic feeling to the delicate, neat lines of the roof and broad balcony. (Sassakawa, Tokyo.)

Plates 26–27. The building and this front entrance garden are closely linked together by the tile-roofed, beige, earthen-plaster wall, whose natural extension is the clipped hedge of *Eurya japonica*. The moss-covered hillock, at approximately the same height as the porch, causes the hedge to appear closer to the house than it actually is. There is a cozy feeling here despite the formality of the geometrical pattern of the cut-stone walk. By planting the hedge on the hillock's elevation, the designer has effectively screened off the view of the building in the background without the necessity of having the hedge disproportionately high and inaccessible. The steppingstones, leading off of the pavement, add a less formal feeling as they wind away in the background. The doorway in the wall gives a brief glimpse of the garden — a mood of lightness and expansiveness. The simple lines of the *oribe* stone lantern with ferns growing at its base also bring more warmth to the scene. A low, spreading plum tree stands at the top of the hillock. (Katsura Imperial Villa, Kyoto.)

Plate 28. An entrance court-yard garden in which water-splashed rocks and pebbles, a mossy stone lantern, a water basin, and plantings of bamboo combine to produce a fresh, cool atmosphere. A wooden water ladle and a pot of tiny white chrysanthemums add a light, human touch. The doorway is framed by a *noren* curtain of twisted strands of rice straw. (Kyoto.)

Plate 29. The entrance garden of an inn. Plants and rock are combined in simple fashion to give the guests a restful feeling as they enter the street gate. For ease of maintenance the ground-cover is composed of the stone pavement surrounded on both sides by gray river gravel and pebbles. The pruned trees at the left are box; those on the right, camellia and sasanqua. Along the path beyond the inner gate are growing clumps of bamboo. The potted plant in the left foreground is sago cycas. A pot of white chrysanthemums is set on the well's bamboo cover. (Kyoto.)

Plate 30. A natural and cut-stone inlaid pavement, dark green moss, gray weathered tile, a white plaster wall, and a few plantings are the components of this Zen temple entrance garden. The low shrubs are *Chloranthus glaber*. The tree on the left is *Ternstroemia japonica*. The natural relationship of garden and structure seems to depend upon the simplicity of the composition, which reflects the ascetic quality of life within the temple. The door of the garden wall and the wood elements of the building are stained a blackish brown. The tiles of the roof and wall are a soft gray interspersed with green lichens. (Daitoku-ji, Kyoto.)

Plate 32. The front garden of this private home uses square and rectangular steppingstones, arranged asymmetrically, relating the angular lines of the house to the ground. The round, sheared azalea bushes temper the architectural formality and serve as linking elements to the purely natural forms of the cryptomerias on the left. Several rocks of weathered texture are set into the ground to connect the steppingstones still further with the naturalistic ingredients. Clumps of bamboo by the front door and in the foreground bring delicacy and brightness into the composition to balance the dark greens of the other plants and the dark grays and blacks of the rock and stone. The groundcover beneath the shrubbery is moss, while the rest of the ground is covered with gray river pebbles. A clump of *Eurya japonica* grows under the bamboo in the foreground. The steppingstones, about fourteen inches wide, are set four inches into the ground, each in a separate thin bed of concrete. Water is regularly sprinkled over the plants, rocks, and ground in the summer. (Sakyo-ku, Kyoto.)

Plate 33. The clumps of black bamboo in the entranceway relate to the vertical elements of the building and garden structures of bamboo. The curved baffle fence is made of split bamboo tied together with wire and non-rotting hemp twine. The rocks of the natural flagstone walk are set in a concrete bed. Their ochre and beige colors match the natural earthen-plaster walls. The ground-cover of black-speckled, white, gravelly sand gives a clean, fresh feeling and is easy to maintain. (Kyoto.)

Plate 34. A flat granite walk with clipped-box hedges on both ▶ sides leads you in a simple, direct way to the front door of this temple. The imposing roof of the building is matched by the bold, round forms of Fortune osmanthus bushes, which contrast well with the straight architectural lines and the sweeping curve of the roof. The tall hinoki cypress is a natural counterpart of the aspiring peaks of the roof. (Myoshin-ji, Kyoto.)

Looking from House to Garden

(Plates 35–67; see text pages 51–52)

Plate 35. This garden is only about twenty-five feet deep. To give it more depth and interest it was made on two slightly different levels divided by a shallow, narrow gully. The rectangular rock on the farther bank is a fragment of ancient stone sculpture of Buddhist images in bas-relief. Framed by the delicate-textured, light-green leaves of the shrub above it and the moss groundcover, the stone become a charming and subtle point of strength and spirituality. (Saga residence, Kanazawa.)

Plate 36. The soft green moss inside the glassed-in terrace is easily and consistently maintained in a luxuriant condition throughout the year. The moss seems almost to flow past the threshold of the rooms, integrating in a striking and unusual way the house with the moss and grass-covered outer garden. The steppingstones and the massive "shoe-removing stone" below the threshold relate closely to the outer rocks and stones. Ferns and a grassy shrub add a delicate naturalism to the mossy terrace. The people who live here sprinkle the moss lightly with a watering can. The outer glass sliding panels are removed in the summer. (Hayashiya residence, Kanazawa.)

Plate 37. The cut-granite slabs set in a line as steppingstones and the mud-plaster wall with a topping of roof tiles give this temple garden strength and stability. The form of the deciduous tree on the left has been wrought by years of pruning. The arrangement of the stone lantern, the evergreen podocarpus, the box shrubs, and rocks vividly illustrates the Japanese concept of asymmetrical balance. (Koho-an, Daitoku-ji, Kyoto.)

Plate 38. The moss garden of a private home on a hilltop overlooking the city. Slight, rhythmic undulations and miniature hillocks in the ground surface increase its interest and variation. The steppingstones and rock groupings, deeply imbedded in the ground, suggest stability and bring a settled, enclosed, secure feeling into the scene. A sheltered garden seat provides a place from which to enjoy the view below. (Nakamura residence, Kanazawa.)

Plate 39. A corner of a private garden with the first winter snow on the ground. The basin for rinsing the hands is made of ancient pottery. The background woven baffle is made of thin strips of hinoki cypress. The tree is maple. (Hirata residence, Hida-Takayama, Gifu Prefecture.)

Plate 40. An inner garden of a temple. The shrubs are broad-leafed evergreens. The groundcover is moss and gravelly sand. As if they were round steppingstones, circles of moss in diminishing size and irregular pattern extend from the veranda out into the sand bed. They relate the round form of the stone water basin to the rest of the garden. (Konchi-in, Nanzen-ji, Kyoto.)

Plate 41. The weathered stone column of an *oribe* stone lantern with the cryptic bas-relief of the Virgin and the initials of the Latin words, *Iesus, Filius Dei*, in the form of a Japanese printed character carved above it. It is set close to the bamboo veranda, and surrounded by cryptomeria and *Ternstroemia japonica* trees. See also Plate 181. (Saga residence, Kanazawa.)

Plate 42. This shallow, narrow temple garden achieves greater perspective by using large-leafed plants near the house and finer textured ones in the background. It would appear even deeper if the back wall were of a darker color. (Shomyo-ji, Nara.)

Plate 43. Stone lanterns and water basins require adjacent elements of the same texture in the ground to give them balance and stability. A translucent screening component is also necessary. Here, one large rock, several smaller ones, and a line of evergreen shrubbery are used. (Koho-an, Daitoku-ji, Kyoto.)

Plate 44. A quiet, simple garden facing the long porch of a Zen temple. Its dominating feature is the Japanese black pine, which has been tenderly pruned over the years so that even its lowest branches are healthy and vigorous. The groundcover is moss. A low two-and-a-half-foot hedge of evergreen oak defines the limits of the garden's plant life. Beyond it stands an earthen-plaster wall. Clipped box and azalea shrubs are planted in an asymmetrical pattern around the pine to give balance and rhythm to the composition. A low, narrow border of *Ardisia crispa* runs partway along the edge of the stone-and-tile paving. (Shinju-an, Daitoku-ji, Kyoto.)

Plate 45. Rounded river stones and rocks lead from the building into the garden, giving needed contrast with the sharp, jutting lines of the trees. Water dripping from a bamboo spout into the rock basin and the wooden ladle humanize the scene. The outsize stone lantern, though slightly grotesque and out of proportion with its surroundings, contrasts powerfully with the natural setting and adds to it a touch of humor. (Doi Inn, Maruyama, Kyoto.)

Plate 46. As you sit on the veranda the high, rounded, billowing forms of the azaleas look like ocean waves rolling into a sandy beach. Above the azeleas hover maples and pines. A white sandy path winds among the shrubbery. Here, by the very power of its rhythmic mass, rather than by transitional, man-made elements, nature enters into the architectural frame. This feeling is heightened by allowing the azaleas to reach the level of the floor of the building. To save you from being engulfed and "drowned," your eyes can cast upon an occasional "buoy" such as a stone lantern. (Doi Inn, Maruyama, Kyoto.)

Plate 47. A path of natural steppingstones in a bed of pebbles laid in front of a garden tea pavilion. The gray cut-granite curbing, about six inches deep, forms a border between the natural shaped rock elements and the lawn, projecting the straight lines of the building into the garden. The angularity of the curbing saves the pavilion from being swallowed up by its naturalistic environment. (Shokintei, Katsura Imperial Villa, Kyoto.)

Plate 48. Correspondence exists here between the rounded river stones set in a concrete bed below the threshold and the larger rounded river rocks used as steppingstones in the garden. Although the inlaid concrete bed is formed in straight lines to match the lines of the house, its interior parts are round, matching the rocks and sheared azalea shrubs in the garden. Both the stones in the concrete and the garden steppingstones are raised up out of their matrices. The garden is shallow, but a feeling of greater depth is achieved by planting tall masking plants near the building, and by arranging the contours of the ground on several slightly undulating levels. (Izumoya, Kyoto.)

Plate 49. The split-bamboo sleeve fence, attached to the wall of the house, curves out into the garden. It establishes a subtle enclosure, yet allows the feeling for the live plant materials on the other side to permeate through. In one sense, the fence is an organic architectural element, while, in another, it is closely akin to the growing plants. The water basin is constructed of flat slabs of natural stone cemented together. The Buddhist stone sculptures carry a further humanistic, spiritual ingredient out into the natural scene. (Tomoda residence, Yamashina, Kyoto.)

Plate 50. The fine-textured shrubs and grasses and the clipped honeysuckle hedge are soft in feeling, contrasting with the wildness of the mountain forest in the background. The mowed lawn with gravel paths, the big parasol and garden furniture make the setting warm and intimate. (Kicho, Arashi-yama, Kyoto.)

Plate 51. The paper-panel doors of this room are slid back allowing nature in the month of March almost to leap inside. It is a mixed planting of evergreen azaleas, sassa bamboo, oak, maples, and flowering trees. A path of steppingstones leads from the edge of the room out into the garden. (Nagai residence, Tokyo.)

Plate 52. The curving split-bamboo fence separates this corner from the rest of the garden. It contains the essential elements of a tea-pavilion garden—stone water basin, lantern, and dust hole to be used as a temporary receptacle for small trash. The rock arrangement around the water basin is held in place by mortar concealed by moss and soil. The basin is set into a depression called a "sea," which is covered with river pebbles. Overflow of water from basins is drained away by concealed pipes leading to porous, sandy soil or to a small pit of buried gravel and sand. (Izumoya, Kyoto.)

Plates 53–54. The straight lines of the cut-granite slabs and the neatness of the white gravelly sand raked in a pattern of billowing waves balance out the hard austerity of the rocks in this temple garden. (Narita Fudo, Osaka Prefecture.)

Plate 55. The joints in the cut-stone slabs, running perpendicular to the line of the building, lead your eyes out into the restrained garden as if pointing the way to follow. The rocks are grouped into a balanced, harmonious composition. The grassy knoll and sheared shrubs and trees in the background blend well with the massive, solid feeling of the rock elements. (Narita Fudo, Osaka Prefecture.)

Plate 56. A courtyard garden whose outer dimensions are nine by twelve feet. Since it is an interior garden, its integration with the building is taken for granted. But the link-up is achieved through subtle artistry. A group of rocks is set in the pavement at a level only slightly lower than the floor of the room. These rocks then relate to a group within the moss-covered center. The delicately textured leaves of the tall maple on the left and the shorter *Podocarpus macrophylla* on the right add a light, soft feeiing to balance the more solid, more coarsely textured elements. The slightly oversize stone lantern, in its off-center position, gives the composition substance and importance. The final effect is one of harmony of texture, weight, and quiet elegance. (Tanimura residence, Kanazawa.)

Plate 57. A teahouse-restaurant garden with lawn and paths, which allow it to be actively used. (Kicho, Arashi-yama, Kyoto.)

Plate 58. A corner in a private garden. The three-and-a-half-foot wide "shoe-removing rock" of weathered granite, at the foot of the veranda, carries the straight line of the house out into the garden. Its soft gray colorings, enhanced by pools of rain water collected in its shallow depressions, give a cool feeling in summer. The water gives it a dynamism. It is set in a sea of gravelly sand, about three inches deep, laid over a bed of hard-tamped earth. Dark, weathered, moss-covered rocks, like islands, jut up out the sand. The rocks are unobtrusive yet important parts of the composition. Lines are raked in the sand to represent water gently rolling against the rocks. Concentric rings raked in the sand represent drops of water falling into a pool, creating ever-widening circles. The straight line of rocks at the far edge of the sand carries the architectural lines still farther out into the garden. The big, reclining mossy rock in the middle distance seems to anchor the other elements to the ground. The sleeve fence is made of the twigs of shrub bush clover and bamboo. A young maple tree and ferns are growing out from the edge of the "shoe-removing stone." The low, dark-leaved plants with little red berries at the edge of the sand are *Ardisia crispa*. The dwarf striped leaves are sassa bamboo grass. Japanese aucuba is planted by the sleeve fence, and a maple stands by the stone lantern. (Watanabe residence, Hida-Furukawa, Gifu Prefecture.)

Plates 59–60. The house and the garden are perched on two terraced levels of a hillside. The groundcover is gravelly sand raked in fine straight lines perpendicular to the line of the house. The neat, sheared azaleas by the house and on the terraced slope convey the idea of human control and architectural strength far out into the distance, fusing and yet separating the garden from the forested background. The sasanqua camellia tree, just outside the threshold, frames the view. Fed by a waterfall at the left near the house, a babbling mountain stream winds among the azaleas. (Shisendo Retreat, Kyoto.)

Plate 61. The concrete terrace in the foreground would ordinarily seem definitely a part of the house, especially since it is sheltered by its broad, overhanging roof. But the link to the garden was made by laying the broad steppingstones in the terrace, half in the concrete and half in the moss-covered soil. The cold, hard line of the pavement is also softened by the border of black and gray river pebbles and stones. The clumps of low-growing, heart-shaped leaves by two of the steppingstones is wild ginger (*Asarum asaroides*). (Nishida residence, Kanazawa.)

Plate 62. A broad, one-piece slab of stone is set just below the threshold of the main room of the house. Large steppingstones carry the stone element farther out. Rounded knolls and hillocks and shallow gullies give depth and mystery to the scene. The sheared shrubs are azalea and box. Clumps of daffodils are naturalized among the rocks. The groundcover is a grass lawn. (Nagai residence, Tokyo.)

Plate 63. The steppingstones lead from the paved terrace out into the depths of the garden, merging naturally into the rocky shoreline of the pond. The undulating surface of the ground gives the illusion of greater depth. (Izumoya, Kyoto.)

Plate 65. The rock element of the inlaid-stone pavement is carried gradually, through the transitional medium of steppingstones and pebbles, out into the garden. A garden stream in a shallow gully, masked here by rocks, ferns, and grasses, trickles among the rocks in the middle ground. (Kaba residence, Hida-Furukawa, Gifu Prefecture.)

Plate 66. Stone water basin set near the bamboo ledge of a temple veranda. The water drips into the basin from the bamboo spout. (Kyoto.)

Looking from Garden to House

(Plates 68–78; see text pages 51–52)

Plate 68. The corner of a teahouse in which the transition from structure to garden is achieved through the position of rocks and steppingstones—the massive "shoe-removing rock" set by the veranda, followed by a flat rock sunk into the moss-covered ground, and then the steppingstones leading out into the garden. The round stone was originally used as the footing stone for one of the thick wooden columns of a temple. A straight border of gray pebbles extends along the ground below the veranda. A narrow tile-paved terrace by the far wall is sheltered by overhanging eaves. A stone water basin, with ferns growing around its base, gives a cool, fresh feeling. The *oribe* stone lantern brings geometrical lines into the garden. Its soft light, partially masked by the branches of the *Ternstroemia japonica* tree, illuminates the path and veranda at night. (Ichi-Riki, Gion, Kyoto.)

Plate 69. A simple courtyard garden in a centuries-old teahouse, approximately fifteen by twenty-one feet. The rocks are set into the moss-covered soil in a naturalistic grouping around a rock water basin, which forms the central point of interest. Cut-granite slabs, about two feet long, and rocks, placed in groups of three and four, compose the steppingstone path leading from the veranda into the garden. The planting is restricted to cryptomeria trees and ferns around the rock basin. The unique shape of the trees is obtained through pruning off the main trunks in the early stages of growth. The limbs, later sprouting out of the stump, are then pruned to get a vertical habit. The garden is surrounded by a high, tile-topped earthen-plaster wall, whose lower portions are covered with a layer of hinoki-cypress bark. A bamboo sleeve fence extends about three feet into the garden from the post separating the two rooms, screening off guests on one side from those on the other. (Ichi-Riki, Gion, Kyoto.)

Plate 70. This is the garden of a novelist's home. What gave it life and vitality? More than anything else it was the placing of the old Buddhist stone carving in this comparatively bare plot of ground. It has spiritual meaning for the man who lives here. He sees it every day and feels some personal identification with it. Against the earth-beige color of the mud-plaster wall, the gravelly sand bed covered with a thin layer of snow, the rocks, and the green lawn and sparse shrubbery make a simple harmony. (Tamura residence, Tokyo.)

Plate 71. Water makes the unity in this garden. The rocky shores of the pond are laid under the very windows of the house. The plum tree's graceful branches provide a living frame for the natural outer scene. (Nagai residence, Tokyo.)

Plate 72. The straight lines of the rock embankment and the hedge above it, sheared at several levels, are factors making the gradual progression from the architectural element to the natural garden environment. (Katsura Imperial Villa, Kyoto.)

Plate 73. The man-made elements—bridges, stone lanterns, steppingstone paths—relate the pavilion to human activity, saving it from isolation and from being lost in the natural landscape. Pruning keeps the plant material under control. (Katsura Imperial Villa, Kyoto.)

Plate 74. The rocks along the footing of the walls are closely related to the rocks in the path. They, in turn, have an affinity with larger rocks set farther away. The main supporting posts are resting on the flat surfaces of large footing-rocks almost completely sunk into the ground. The size and depth of the post footing-rocks are dictated by the weight they must bear and the severity of winter ground frost. The natural texture of the corner supporting columns matches in feeling the trees growing in the garden. (Kicho, Arashi-yama, Kyoto.)

Plate 75. The mixed hedge of slow-growing evergreen oak and box is approximately six feet high and three feet wide. It takes about five years to bring it to the condition shown here. Its geometrical lines, matching the lines of the building, effectively separate it from its natural environment. At the same time, the hedge's color and texture permit it to blend into the surrounding plant material. (Shokintei, Katsura Imperial Villa, Kyoto.) ·

Plate 76. The water of a garden pond, led under the very floors of this tea pavilion, closely ties the building to the site, yet each maintains its own character. The stone water basin, supplying water for guests to rinse their hands, stands in the water. As you bend down to get the water you see your face reflected in the pond. A thin bridge of planks, laid on their edges and bound together, links the two banks of the pond. The round, clipped azalea shrubs and the feathery branches of the pine stretching over the water give a soft and gentle feeling. (Sambo-in, Daigo, Kyoto.)

Plate 77. Water and rock are vigorous links between the house and the garden. One end of the veranda rests on columns set on rocks sunk in the bed of the pond. A thin rivulet rushes down a rocky cascade into the pond at the edge of the house. From the veranda you see and hear the water. (Ichida Villa, Kyoto.)

Plate 78. The curving configuration of the white sand in this temple garden conveys the feeling of a shallow, meandering stream. (Manshu-in, Kyoto.)

Water Features

(Plates 79–100; see text pages 31–33)

Plates 79–80. The steppingstones and pebbles stretched across the neck of sand are arranged to simulate the stones of a real stream. The water current is raked into the sand. (Tomoda residence, Yamashina, Kyoto.)

Plate 81. A murmuring garden stream with a crossing rock set in the water course. Naturalized plantings of maple, azalea, fern, Japanese andromeda, box, and *Ternstroemia japonica* are set along the moss-covered banks. (Imperial Palace, Kyoto.)

Plate 82. Steppingstones connecting a path which leads across a garden stream. It is a welcome feeling to walk across water with dry feet, hearing its gurgle and seeing it flowing only a few inches away. In summer it is hard to resist stooping down to wet your hands in the cool water. Ferns, grasses, and a shrubby willow grow along the banks. (Murin-an, Kyoto.)

122

Plate 83. Steppingstones across a stream. The water swirls over low cataracts just below your feet. (Tatsumura Silk House, Kyoto.)

Plate 84. The low shoreline of a shallow garden stream in which rocks along the edges are arranged as subordinate elements to the planting of low, sheared azaleas, ferns, moss, and grass. The effect is that of a sunny meadow where the influence of man is barely felt. (Murin-an, Kyoto.)

Plate 85. A broad, shallow stream with rocks set in along the banks. A bamboo frame supports the limbs of the Japanese red pine pruned in the form of a parasol. (Imperial Palace, Kyoto.)

Plate 86. A shallow stream with grassy banks planted with low, spreading azaleas sheared in gentle, rounded forms. The few scattered rocks play a minor role; the emphasis here is on the plant materials. (Ichida Villa, Kyoto.)

Plate 87. A narrow garden streamlet with precipitous rocky banks symbolizing a deep mountain ravine. From the bed of the stream to the top of the upper rocks is only about twenty inches, yet the artful handling of scale gives the impression of a vast and deep canyon. (Ginkaku-ji, Kyoto.)

Plate 88. The width of a garden stream depends on the factors of scale of the house and garden and the quantity of water available. The gradient of a murmuring streamlet should be at least three to one hundred. Here, the stream is composed of a series of low, rocky steps over which the water pours in a zigzag fashion around the larger, taller rocks and over the shallow ones. (Tatsumura Silk House, Kyoto.)

Plate 89. The rapids cause the water to splash as it drops among the rocks. The bed of the stream is clay overlaid with river sand and pebbles. Rocks of different heights and contours are set deeply into the stream bed and arranged so that the water is split into rivulets which seek the lower gradient through the spaces between the rocks. Plantings of ferns and moss are set in rock crevices and along the banks. (Imperial Palace, Kyoto.)

Plate 90. A boat landing built up of cut, gray granite at the water's edge of a garden pond. The stone lantern is appropriately placed to illuminate the spot at night. Note the two clumps of iris—one on the shore and the other in the water. (Katsura Imperial Villa, Kyoto.)

Plate 91. Dark gray river stones extend above and below the waterline of this boat landing. Stepping-stones lead from a garden path to the landing. (Imperial Palace, Kyoto.)

Plate 92. Another boat landing. Charred pilings about two inches in diameter are sunk into the bed of the pond at the ends of the cut-stone steps. When the landing stones are flush with the shoreline, natural, projecting rocks are set at both ends of the cut stone. (Imperial Palace, Kyoto.)

Plate 93. An old maple, a broadleafed evergreen shrub, moss, rocks, and a stone lantern compose this shoreline detail by a garden pond. The rocks are carefully set into the higher embankment with part of their weight supported by larger rocks lower down the slope and in the pond bed. (Katsura Imperial Villa, Kyoto.)

Plate 94. Massive rocks, sand mounds, and earth are the dominating elements, overshadowing the plants. The rocks are grouped as symbolic expressions of natural landscapes. The garden has a rough, coarse texture and feeling which seems in sharp contrast to the delicacy of the architectural elements. It gives a dose of ruggedness and strength to what would otherwise seem to be only the fleeting whim or caprice of the dilettante esthete prince who built it 700 years ago as an escape from the cares of his office. The rocks projecting above the surface of the water rest on deeply embedded bolster rocks below the water's surface. Even if the pond is drained or should dry up, the rocky shoreline will not crumble and erode but will retain its form and interest. (Ginkaku-ji, Kyoto.)

Plate 95. A wooden pavilion over a neck of water of a garden pond. The columns rest on rocks which in turn are set on larger rocks sunk into the bed of the pond. According to ancient practice in such construction, the distance between the water surface and the underside of the beam supporting the hurdle of the pavilion should be at least five inches. Note that the point of land is built up with larger rocks, while the cove has only moss, and a few small rocks and ferns planted right to the water's edge. (Kodai-ji, Kyoto.)

Plate 96. The twisting, rocky shoreline of a garden pond with a Japanese andromeda shrub at the right. The isolated rock set out in the water is a focus of interest and imparts a feeling of greater distance. It serves as a kind of pivot rock or fulcrum causing the background to seem to shift as you move along the opposite bank. High, grassy reeds grow out of the rock chinks, which are filled with soil. Such isolated rocks should be supported by three bolster rocks grouped in the form of a tripod embedded deeply in the bottom of the pond. The isolated rock is usually set out into the water about thirty inches from a point of land which has large rocks of the same color and texture. This gives the impression that at one time it was part of the rocky point, but became separated in the process of natural erosion. (Kodai-ji, Kyoto.)

Plate 97. The shoreline of a garden pond. The rock element is strongest on the peninsula and jutting points of land, and weakest at the coves and indentations. (Tenryu-ji, Arashi-yama, Kyoto.)

Plate 98. A woodland garden pond in which thick moss covers the ground and seems to flow down to the shoreline. The rocks set in a line in the water add a human touch to the otherwise almost purely naturalistic setting. Many varieties of moss, maple, oak, pine, cypress, and cryptomeria are growing here. (Saiho-ji, Kyoto.)

Plate 99. A double waterfall from a series of two cliffs made in a garden with a constant and cheap source of water supply. (Tatsumura Silk House, Kyoto.)

Plate 100. One way to get a stream in your garden without using much water. The force is gravity. The water drips and flows through a series of bamboo pipes, finally ending up in a stone basin. (Akaza residence, Uchinada, Ishikawa Prefecture.)

Enclosures

(Plates 101–135; see text pages 34–39)

Plate 101. A split-bamboo fence set on a two-foot-high retaining wall of cut-granite and concrete. Young evergreen oaks provide a delicate contrast to the strong sharp lines of the white plaster *okura* storehouse at the edge of this private garden. (Sakyo-ku, Kyoto.)

Plate 102. Bamboo is used in three different ways in the fence and gate. The frame of the fence on the left is covered with a lateral stacking of thin bamboo stalks and twigs. The gate is made of bamboo which was split, while still green, into thin tapelike lengths and then woven over the gate frame. The fence portion on the right is made of thin bamboo poles tied to horizontal poles. (Tomoda residence, Yamashina, Kyoto.)

Plate 103. Here is the other side of the same fence. Instead of bamboo twigs, it is finished in split bamboo.

Plate 104. A low, delicate, graceful bamboo fence set over a rock footing in a temple garden. (Ryoan-ji, Kyoto.)

139

Plate 105. A split-bamboo fence leading away from a wall of the house. (Tomoda residence, Yamashina, Kyoto.)

Plate 106. A split-bamboo fence, about three feet high, on a two-and-a-half-foot-high rock retaining wall, topped by a seven-foot clipped hedge of evergreen oak on the left and camellia on the right. It is the entrance walk of the Silver Pavilion. Such imposing forms as these towering hedges are only appropriate when the garden is built on a grand scale or when a strong element, showing cultivated, human effects, is needed to counterbalance an outside, dominating, naturalistic element—in this case, a mountain in the background, towering over the garden. The delicate line and color of the bamboo fence soften the feeling. (Ginkaku-ji, Kyoto.)

Plate 107. A combination of bamboo fence and clipped shrubby yew podocarpus hedge built on a stone retaining wall along the street side of a private home. (Kyoto.)

Plate 108. A split-bamboo fence made on two levels. The rock rampart is a remnant of an ancient wall. (Kyoto.)

Plate 109 A bamboo gate in a two-hundred-year-old design. The gate posts are of sturdy, unpainted logs sunk deep into the soil. (Shugakuin Imperial Villa.)

Plate 110. A *shiorido* bamboo garden fence and gate. Evergreen oak and a clinging vine grow through the fence. The bamboo posts and horizontal members are bound together with thin wire and non-rotting twine. The gate is made of thin, split bamboo formed on a bamboo frame and laid in the form of a grill tied together with twine. A broad, flat-topped steppingstone is set into the ground just beneath the gate. (Ura Senke, Kyoto.)

Plate 111. The fence of this private home is composed of bundles of shrub bush clover twigs and branches tied together with wire and twine. The bundles are lashed to horizontal bamboo poles, which are in turn tied to heavier posts set deep into the ground. The pattern of the twig bundles alternates, with three outside and three inside. A narrow roof of cedar-bark shingles set on a wooden frame is erected over the fence to protect it from the rotting effects of too much moisture. (Kyoto.)

Plate 112. This private home has a street fence of two layers of thin bamboo twigs tied to a bamboo pole frame. The complete structure is stabilized by heavy posts sunk in the rock-and-concrete footing. A wooden roof protects the fence from rotting due to rain. (Kyoto.)

Plate 114. A wooden garden gate and grilled fence, though defining the garden's limits, at the same time allows some feeling of the outside elements to penetrate into the garden. It is a gentle, subtle enclosure. Below the grill are panels of beige mud plaster. The gate and fence are roofed with gray tile. The unpainted wood elements weather to a soft gray. (Saami, Kyoto.)

Plates 115–116. Two garden fences that face the street. They are set on solid rock footings. The boards and posts are unpainted and have weathered to a soft gray. The upper portions are earthen plaster topped by a protective tile roofing. The grills are of slender bamboo. They let some of the outside in and often some of the inside out. These seven-foot-high fences afford privacy, while the grills prevent claustrophobia. (Silver Pavilion Road, Kyoto.)

Plate 117. The interior garden of a private home in the month of November. The walls are covered with split black bamboo, woven cypress shingling, and beige earthen plaster. The effect is one of soberness, restraint, and elegance. (Hirata residence, Takayama, Gifu Prefecture.)

Plate 118. The street fence of a private home, set on a cut-granite palisade. The fence is made of woven strips of cedar wood supported on a wood-post frame. It is topped by a narrow roofing of tiles (Kyoto.)

Plate 119. The wall of the house is covered with ochre bamboo. Stalks of green and yellow bamboo blend with the wall. A planting of yew is in the foreground. (Akaza residence, Uchinada, Ishikawa Prefecture.)

Plate 120. The white-washed plaster wall of a temple several centuries old. The grill design suggests Indian and Moslem influences. The interior of each square is painted a flat black. (Higashi Hongan-ji, Kyoto.)

Plate 121.   The white mud-plaster walls of a temple, resting on a firm footing of a rock parapet. A tile roof keeps the plaster dry. (Manpuku-ji, Uji, Kyoto.)

Plate 122. A dobe earthen-plaster wall, five feet high and whitewashed.
It is built on a solid, broad rampart of rock. (Saiho-ji, Kyoto.)

Plate 123. A temple wall of white-washed mud plaster mixed with straw, topped by a narrow tile roof. The doorway is an old Chinese arch. (Tenryu-ji, Arashi-yama, Kyoto.)

Plate 124. A garden wall of white-washed mud-and-straw plaster panels. The wood beams are stained a dark brown. The wall is topped with tiles. (Senryu-ji, Kyoto.)

Plate 125. Detail of a mud plaster and rice-straw wall. The lower border is composed of old roof tiles set into the plaster. (Kyoto.)

Plate 126. A wall of earthen-brown plaster in which were placed fragments of old temple roof tiles. (Tenryu-ji, Arashi-yama, Kyoto.)

Plate 127. Shrubby yew podocarpus hedge of a teahouse. (Enri-an, Saga, Kyoto.)

Plate 128. A low clipped hedge of *Ternstroemia japonica* encloses this modest grouping of seven rocks and several azaleas. The ground-cover is moss. (Shinju-an, Daitoku-ji, Kyoto.)

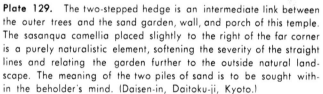

Plate 129. The two-stepped hedge is an intermediate link between the outer trees and the sand garden, wall, and porch of this temple. The sasanqua camellia placed slightly to the right of the far corner is a purely naturalistic element, softening the severity of the straight lines and relating the garden further to the outside natural landscape. The meaning of the two piles of sand is to be sought within the beholder's mind. (Daisen-in, Daitoku-ji, Kyoto.)

Plate 130. A sleeve-fence at the corner of a house screens off what is not to be seen. It is made of bundles of slender bamboo twigs and branches. (Tamura residence, Kyoto.)

Plate 131. A narrow sleeve-fence of twisted, dark-brown hemp in a bamboo frame. (Tomoda residence, Yamashina, Kyoto.)

Plate 132. A simple bamboo sleeve-fence merges with the bamboo elements of the building itself. (Myoki-an, Yamazaki Kyoto.)

Plate 133. A roofed garden gate whose two sturdy posts retain their natural bark. The doors of the gate are made of bamboo. The roof is thatched with rice straw. The bamboo fence is intertwined with pruned evergreen oak to add a dynamic feeling and a texture which blends with the natural environment yet provides an effective baffle. (Katsura Imperial Villa, Kyoto.)

Plate 134. The street wall and gate of a teahouse-restaurant. The combination of white plaster and clapboard repeats the materials of the building. (Saami, Kyoto.)

Plate 135. Inside the front gate of a teahouse. (Enri-an, Saga, Kyoto.)

Steppingstones & Pavements

(Plates 136–171; see text pages 40–41)

◀ **Plate 136.** Steppingstones of a path leading through the garden of an extensive villa. Seven-eighths of the stone is firmly embedded in the soil. The axis of each stone is perpendicular to the axis of the path. Three to four inches of space are between the stones. Generally a stone is laid so that a convex side adjoins a concave edge of the following stone. The surface of each stone is level, thus giving a feeling of stability to the stroller. A layer of gray river pebbles provides a change of feeling and a fresh contrast with the moss and grass surrounding other stretches of the path. The pebbles also link the steppingstones with the rocky shoreline along which the path runs. Since the path is on a slope, at each step you see a changing scene from a slightly different angle. (Katsura Imperial Villa, Kyoto.)

Plate 137. An irregular pattern of rounded steppingstones set in a groundcover of deep moss. (Tsuruya, Kyoto.)

Plate 138. Round steppingstones set in a lawn leading to a garden teahouse. The round hillock covered with ivy and pachysandra gives a sense of greater depth to the scene. The tall, reedy plant in the pond is a scouring rush (*Equisetum hyemale*), an especially hardy evergreen. (Chinzanso, Tokyo.)

◄ **Plate 140.** Walking along this path of steppingstones, your interest is enlivened as you descend from the moss background to that of the river pebbles. The stones and pebbles create a freshness, a tonic astringency to counterbalance the mass of greenery. (Katsura Imperial Villa, Kyoto.)

Plate 141. Oblong and square steppingstones set in a pattern which is practical for walking. They are raised about one quarter of an inch above the surface of the pebbles to allow for water drainage. (Kyoto.)

Plate 142. A walk of square granite slabs and curbing in which moss has grown up between the stones. (Nanzen-ji, Kyoto.)

Plate 143. Steppingstones in a Zen temple garden. (Marishi-ten, Nanzen-ji, Kyoto.)

Plate 144. Flat, granite flagstones, three inches thick, make for ▶ easy walking and contrast strongly with the natural features of the building and garden. The moss looks ragged in the winter but in the spring becomes thick and luxuriant again. (Tomoda residence, Yamashina, Kyoto.)

Plate 145. A walk of gray granite steppingstones set in a bed of white, gravelly sand. It provides a strong, logical progression from the line of the building to the evergreen oak hedge and the back wall. (Hojo, Daitoku-ji, Kyoto.)

Plate 146. Looking from inside the front door. The floor of the vestibule is paved with rounded river stones set in concrete, providing a change of feeling from the rectangular stones between the gate and the front door. (Tomoda residence, Yamashina, Kyoto.)

Plate 147. Gray granite steppingstones, fifteen inches square and six inches thick, lead you past the pavilion. The geometrical lines of the building are brought into the natural setting by the angularity of the stones placed in an irregular pattern in the moss-covered earth. A twelve-inch-wide border of black river pebbles, pressed into the surface of a sandy soil trough, makes a gentle transition between the strong lines of the stone border around the building and the square steppingstones. The pebbles also serve the practical purpose of catching the rainwater from the edge of the roof, thus eliminating puddles. (Katsura Imperial Villa, Kyoto.)

Plate 148. Natural and cut-stone pavement set ▶ in a bed of concrete six inches deep. (Kyoto.)

Plate 149. Stone pavement and steppingstones combined in a garden path. An easier transition is achieved by using in the pavement rocks of approximately the same shape, size, color, and texture as those of the linking steppingstones which connect with it. (Katsura Imperial Villa, Kyoto.)

Plate 150. A pavement laid in a mortar bed about ▶ eight inches thick. (Katsura Imperial Villa, Kyoto.)

Plate 151. An entrance walk set in a bed of mortar. (Minoko, Kyoto.)

Plate 152. Granite slabs and natural rocks set in a mortar matrix. (Chinzanso, Tokyo.)

Plate 153. A garden pavement, made on a gentle gradient, composed of natural rocks and cut-granite slabs set about four inches into a bed of concrete. The ground on both sides of the walk is covered with fine river gravel. Lengths of split bamboo are bent into semi-circular shape to form a low fence. Shade is provided by a grove of bamboo which rustles in the wind. (Chinzanso, Tokyo.) ▶

Plates 154–155. Natural and cut-stone pavements in a temple courtyard. (Kurodani, Kyoto.)

Plate 156. An entrance walk of granite curbing and river rocks in a ten-inch concrete bed. (Kyoto.)

Plate 157. A natural-rock walk curbed with granite slabs five inches in the ground. (Daitoku-ji, Kyoto.)

Plate 158. The stone walk is set about five inches into the soil. No mortar is used. (Myoshin-ji, Kyoto.)

Plate 159. Tiles laid flat, bordered by granite curbstones, make this pavement in a temple garden. (Ryoan-ji, Kyoto.)

Plate 160. The gravelly sand bed of an intermittent stream fed from the house water main. The paved path is of old roof tiles set in a concrete bed. (Ishida residence, Sakurai, Osaka Prefecture.)

Plate 162. Pavement of roof tiles and stone set in a concrete bed
in a garden of a private home. (Yamashina, Kyoto.)

Plate 164. A broad garden walk composed of gray river pebbles pressed into a shallow mortar bed. The spaces between the pebbles are darkened with mossy earth. The clipped hedge is a mixture of camellia, box, and other evergreen shrubs. It frames the background view and introduces into the garden the feeling of architecture and human control. (Katsura Imperial Villa, Kyoto.)

Plate 165. Cut-granite slabs, about twelve inches square and four inches thick, set into the ground, forming a checkerboard pattern with the moss which has been planted around them. This use of stone and moss makes an interesting groundcover element showing gradual progression from the building to the site. As the stones extend farther into the garden they become fewer and fewer, the moss or grass becoming the dominant groundcover element. (Tofuku-ji, Kyoto.)

Plate 167. Steppingstones, leading across a corner of a pond, connecting two sections of a stroll garden. The rocks are set deep into the bottom of the pond with just their broad, flat surfaces exposed about two inches above the water's surface. You feel safe and stable when you walk across them. The path leads into a grove of *Cunninghamia sinensis*. (Tatsumura Silk House, Kyoto.)

Plate 168. Cut-granite block combined with natural rocks to form steppingstones connecting a garden path. (Imperial Palace, Kyoto.)

Plate 169. Old millstones laid across a garden stream. (Tatsumura Silk House, Kyoto.)

193

Plate 170. A path of steppingstones set along the shoreline of a garden stream leading to a stone water basin set into the bed of the stream. The planting around the basin is a species of live oak. (Murin-an, Kyoto.)

Plate 171. Steppingstones crossing a stream in a park. (Korakuen, Okayama.)

Artifacts

(Plates 172–234; see text pages 42–45)

Plate 172. A lichen-covered stone lantern in the shape of a farm cottage. It rests on a shallow rock footing surrounded by a mossy turf at the edge of a pond. The round and crescent windows represent the sun and the moon. A candle or a primitive type of oil lamp, consisting of a burning wick in a dish of oil, is inserted into the lantern. It gives a flickering light which is soft and elusive as seen from the opposite shore. To keep the wind from blowing out the flame, paper windows mounted on thin wooden frames are fitted into the lantern's apertures. (Katsura Imperial Villa, Kyoto.)

Plate 173. Stone lantern perched on a rocky point at the end of a peninsula in a garden pond. (Katsura Imperial Villa, Kyoto.)

Plate 174. A stone lantern set on a rock along an oak-and-azalea-covered shore of a pond. (Joju-in, Kiyomizu-dera, Kyoto.)

Plate 175. A weathered stone lantern, with plantings of fern and *Eurya ochnacea*, placed at the turn of a garden path. (Katsura Imperial Villa, Kyoto.)

Plate 176. A Kasuga stone lantern with plantings of dwarf bamboo in a corner of a private garden. (Tomoda residence, Yamashina, Kyoto.)

Plate 177. A Kasuga type of stone lantern designed by Tansai Sano, Kyoto.

Plate 178. Stone lantern by a pond surrounded by azalea and evergreen oak. (Joju-in, Kiyomizu-dera, Kyoto.)

Plate 179. An *oribe* lantern in a temple garden. (Koho-an, Daitoku-ji, Kyoto.)

Plate 180. *Oribe* lantern. (Katsura Imperial Villa, Kyoto.)

Plate 181. The *oribe* style of stone lantern, designed over two hundred years ago, has a religious association with Christianity. Although Christianity was proscribed during the three hundred years of the Tokugawa shogunate, many Japanese who had been converted by Portuguese and Spanish Jesuit priests continued to practice their religion secretly, resorting to various camouflages to fool the authorities. The *oribe* stone lanterns, set in the gardens of those crypto-Christians, not only differed in design from other styles of stone lanterns, but also in its essential spirit. The bas-relief carved in its base, though disguised as a Buddhist image, was in reality that of the Virgin Mary. See also Plate 41. (Hanjo Jinja, Kyoto.)

Plate 182. A garden lamp made in a granite post. The frosted glass is set in a hinged wooden frame. (Kyoto.)

Plate 183. A garden lantern of wood and frosted glass set on a bamboo pole and lighted by electricity conducted by underground wires. (Chinzanso, Tokyo.)

Plate 184. Iron lanterns of the Tokugawa period hanging from the eaves of a Kyoto temple.

Plate 185. *Rengeji stone lantern and water basin. (Seiren-in Kyoto.)*

Plate 186. A lichen-covered stone water basin and lantern, placed at the end of a flagstone garden pavement, is a point of interest, and suggests human activity associated with the use of water and artificial light. It thus softens the strong massive feeling of the pavement and adjacent rocks. The large rock in front of the basin, with its axis perpendicular to that of the pavement, makes a kind of stop sign or termination point. The basin, of course, also provides a source of water which guests use to rinse their hands while waiting in the pavilion for the tea ceremony call. (Katsura Imperial Villa, Kyoto.)

Plates 187–188. Water basin and stone lantern in a teahouse garden. (Shinju-an, Daitoku-ji, Kyoto.)

Plate 189.   A stone water basin standing by the verandá of a private home. A medieval oil lantern of iron hangs from the eaves. (Shokado, Kyoto.)

Plate 190. An arrangement of stone water basin, lantern, rocks, and tile fragments surrounded by a sea of moss. (Akaza residence, Uchinada, Ishikawa Prefecture.)

Plate 191. Moss-covered basin, lantern, and rocks.
(Nishida residence, Kanazawa.)

Plate 192. Stone basin and lantern.
(Katsura Imperial Villa, Kyoto.)

Plate 193. A round stone basin with a square-cut water receptacle, designed to resemble the face of an old Japanese coin. (Ryoan-ji, Kyoto.)

Plate 194. A carved-stone water basin set along-side a path of steppingstones. Groundcover is fine, soft, green moss. (Kawada residence, Kanazawa.)

Plate 195. A rectangular stone water basin by the side of a gar den pavilion. Its outer dimensions are roughly twenty by fifteen by fifteen inches. It is linked in feeling to the building through the use of square and oblong black stones set into the ground in front of it. It is surrounded by a shallow bed of river pebbles which relate to a similar element around the structure. The water in the basin relates to a farther landscape feature—the garden pond. (Katsura Imperial Villa, Kyoto.)

Plate 196. Stone water basin on a short stone column in a temple garden. (Kyoto.)

Plate 197. A stone basin at the corner of a building. It is replenished by water brought to it in a pail. The ground is completely moss covered. The rock surfaces have turned a soft green. (Obai-in, Daitoku-ji, Kyoto.)

Plate 198. A stone water basin in
a temple garden. (Manshu-in, Kyoto.)

Plate 199. A stone water basin set just off the sidewalk by the front door of a restaurant. Guests may rinse their hands before entering. An iron pipe runs up inside the bamboo spout. The basin is set in concrete overlaid with pebbles and rock which conceal a drain pipe. In the soil area are growing leatherleaf mahonia, box, Japanese eurya, and scouring rush, all hardy in city conditions. A narrow sleeve fence of shrub bush clover twigs provides a natural, rustic background. The metal rail in the foreground holds shutters which are put up at night when the shop closes. (Shijo-dori, Gion, Kyoto.)

Plate 200. A stone basin with bamboo spout by a garden teahouse. Moss and clumps of bamboo grass are planted around it. (Watanabe residence, Hida-Furukawa, Gifu Prefecture.)

Plate 201. A *tsukubai* basin and ''sea'' by a path in a tea garden. (Ishida residence, Sakurai, Osaka Prefecture.)

Plate 202. A bas-relief stone carving in a temple garden. (Daikaku-ji, Saga, Kyoto.)

Plate 203. Buddhist stone sculpture in a corner of a small rear garden, seen against the background of a bamboo fence and simple, sparse plantings of maple, coral ardisia, and camellia. Groundcover is moss and pebbles. (Aihara residence, Fushimi, Kyoto.)

Plate 204. The weathered column of an *oribe* stone lantern with its *María* bas-relief. (Kawada residence, Kanazawa.)

Plate 205. A carved-stone Buddhist figure perched on a rock in a private garden. (Tomoda residence, Yamashina, Kyoto.)

Plate 206. Shrubs and trees, partially masking the stone pagoda set away from the house, enhance the feeling of distance and mystery. (Tatsumura Silk House, Kyoto.)

Plate 207. A two-span arched bridge of cut-stone slabs adjacent to ▶ the veranda of a temple. In the distance, partly masked by shrubbery, stands a stone garden pagoda. Pagodas of nine or thirteen tiers are suitable for high points in the garden. They should be partially masked by plantings of fir, cedar, pine, or cryptomeria. The shorter pagodas of three or five tiers are better set in lighter thickets in lower places or by the shore of a pond to take advantage of the interest in their reflection in the water. (Seiren-in, Kyoto.)

Plate 208. A well in a temple garden. Rocks are usually set by a well to make a balanced, harmonious composition and for practical reasons. The front rock is to stand on, while a flat side stone should be set so that a pail of water can be conveniently placed on it. (Kyoto.)

Plate 209. A well in the garden of a private home. A bamboo cover keeps the water clean. (Kyoto.)

Plate 210. A strong but delicately designed, two-plank bridge over a shallow garden stream. It is set on six unpainted posts set deeply into the clay bed of the stream. The three cross joists are set into the vertical columns. The bridge's zigzag shape causes you to slow down, pause, and enjoy the scene. (Imperial Palace, Kyoto.)

Plate 211. A *yatsu-hashi*, eight-span wooden bridge, used to span a pond or broad, shallow stream where emphasis is on delicacy rather than on sturdiness to stand up to a strong current. The zigzag course forces you to slow down. It makes you take your time, almost insisting that you look at the lotus and iris growing here in the spring and summer. (Korakuen, Okayama.)

Plate 212. Bridge over a pond inlet in a temple garden. (Chishaku-in, Kyoto.)

Plate 213. Low stone bridge over a pond inlet. "Anchor rocks" are not needed here because the bridge is small and close to the water. (Katsura Imperial Villa, Kyoto.)

Plate 214. A massive, one-piece stone bridge across a broad stream. The "anchor rocks" are of proportionate size. This is an extensive palace garden. If the same breadth of water were to be bridged in a modest home garden, the problem of scale, proportion, and feeling would forbid the use of such massive rocks. Instead, thinner stone slabs made into a two-span bridge, or a wooden bridge, would be more appropriate. The planting here is *Pinus parviflora, Podocarpus macrophylla*, red pine, maples, azaleas, and other smaller plants. (Imperial Palace, Kyoto.)

Plate 215. A cut-granite slab used as a bridge. (Ginkaku-ji, Kyoto.)

◄ **Plate 216.** A single-span rock bridge where the rounded forms of sheared box and azalea take the place of "anchor rocks." The tall, clipped shrub in the background is a species of evergreen oak. (Imperial Palace, Kyoto.)

Plate 217. Short arched bridge over a ► narrow streamlet. (Imperial Palace, Kyoto.)

Plate 218. A low, natural-rock bridge with unobtrusive "anchor rocks." The plant materials are a mixture of evergreen azalea, box, oak and moss, and deciduous maples, ferns, and high Japanese silver grass (*Miscanthus*). (Imperial Palace, Kyoto.)

Plate 219.   A graceful, slightly arched, one-piece stone-slab bridge. (Shokintei, Katsura Imperial Villa.)

Plate 220. A two-span stone bridge spanning a pond inlet. The middle rock supports the spans at the center. The "anchor rocks" are supported by large bolster rocks beneath the surface of the water. (Ginkaku-ji, Kyoto.)

Plate 221. A two-span stone bridge supported in the center by cut-granite cross joist and pillars. Anchor and bolster rocks hold up the ends of the bridge. The large leathery-leafed plant in the right foreground is Japanese pittisporum. (Imperial Palace, Kyoto.)

Plate 222. A stone bridge supported by two rocks set in the water. (Chishaku-in Kyoto.)

Plate 223. A two-span bridge of double cut-stone slabs ▶ supported by stone beams and columns. (Ryoan-ji, Kyoto.)

Plate 224. A three-span wooden bridge with two jogs in its axis, supported by five pairs of columns in the water. (Korakuen, Okayama.)

Plate 225. The pavement of this bridge is composed of a base of logs overlaid with packed earth and covered with white sand. It is preferred to hide as much as possible of the foundations of arched bridges. (Imperial Palace, Kyoto.)

Plate 226. A courtyard garden, about twenty by fifteen feet in a Zen temple. The elements of its composition—a groundcover of coarse, white, gravelly sand, raked in a flowing wave pattern, enclosed by granite stone borders and gray tile and river pebbles. Within the garden there is a grouping of lichen-covered rocks with moss growing around their bases. An ascetically pruned camellia tree, tufts of an evergreen grass, and a low box hedge at the far end complete the composition, giving it some slight warmth and softness. (Daisen-in, Daitoku-ji, Kyoto.)

Plate 227. A pattern of wavy, undulating, and straight lines raked into the sand of this Zen temple garden. The rest of the groundcover is moss and shrubbery of pruned maple and pine and clipped evergreen oak and azalea. (Nanzen-ji Hojo, Kyoto.)

Plate 228. A composition of three shades and textures used as ground cover for a border by the porch of a Zen temple garden—the pebbles are closest to the building; next the white granite curbing; and then the sand raked in straight rows. (Nanzen-ji, Kyoto.)

Plate 229. A pattern of straight raked lines in a temple sand garden. At one end of the plot, an eighteen-inch border is raked into lines running perpendicular to the main pattern. (Tenryu-ji, Arashi-yama, Kyoto.)

Plate 230. A combination of ave patterns, straight lines, and two piles of sand in this Zen garden, adjoining the temple portico. The double-tiered hedge is a Japanese privet. (Daisen-in, Daitoku-ji, Kyoto.)

Plate 231. An abstract pattern raked in the sand of
a garden facing a temple porch. (Kennin-ji, Kyoto.)

Plate 232. Portion of a private garden representing a swirling river by the water-current patterns raked into the gravelly sand. (Tomoda residence, Yamashina, Kyoto.)

Plate 233. An abstract composition of attenuated island-like hillocks covered with deep green moss set in a sea of gravelly sand. The standing-rock elements impart a dynamic feeling to the scene. The large tree in the middle ground is a flowering plum tree which blooms in the late summer. Off to the right foreground stands a gracefully branched persimmon tree whose fruit adds color in the fall and early winter. The patterns in the sand convey the feeling of waves and billows of the ocean. (Gasentei, Tomita Villa, Kyoto.)

Plate 234 A mysterious, haunting sound is created by this garden water device. A thin stream of water pours from a bamboo pipe into the open end of a fifteen-inch length of bamboo set on a pivot. As the bamboo fills up with water, its balance is altered and it tips forward on its pivot to empty itself of the water. Having emptied itself, it is restored to its original balance and falls back to its former position, sharply striking a block of wood. The resulting hollow clack echoes regularly through the garden. The bamboo fills up with water again and the process is repeated. (Shisendo Retreat, Kyoto.)

Plate 235. A Japanese red pine on a sloping hillside. Its graceful, gnarled form has been achieved through pruning during its earliest growth. Its drooping branches need the support of wooden poles lashed to the branches. The poles are weathered gray or fire-charred to give a feeling of rusticity and to blend with the dark bark of the tree. (Chinzanso, Tokyo.)

Plate 236. Bamboo poles supporting the limb of a pine tree. (Rokuo-in, Saga, Kyoto.)

Plate 237. A simple teahouse garden with groundcover of moss and plantings of *Ternstroemia japonica* and *Podocarpus macrophylla*. The *kurumazukashi* type of pruning on the podocarpus thins out the branches so that they grow in a habit of separate layers. Since sunlight can penetrate through the entire tree, even the lowest branches remain alive. (Shinju-on, Daitoku-ji, Kyoto.)

Plate 238. Winter wrapping of rice-straw matting to protect the sago cycas here from frost and snow. Because of the natural texture and color of the wrapping, the effect is pleasing. It presents an interesting sculptural form. The low, clipped azalea bushes grouped around the taller plants give the composition balance and stability. (Prefectural Courthouse, Kyoto.)

Plate 239. Rice-straw skirts protect these sago cycas from winter cold. The matting is cheap and has pleasant color and texture. (Katsura Imperial Villa, Kyoto.)

PART FOUR

Plant List

THE TREES, shrubs, vines, and herbaceous plants listed here, by their scientific and common English names, are cultivated by nurseries in North America. Japanese names have been added only in those cases where there is general agreement by Japanese authorities on corresponding nomenclatures. Many species not commonly found in Japan have also been included because they are so appropriate and attractive in naturalistic settings that, in the author's opinion, if they existed in Japan, they would be used in Japanese gardens.

It is a representative list, not meant to be exhaustive and all-inclusive. Each variety listed here has been tried and tested, and is considered both the hardiest of its particular species or family, as well as especially appropriate for planting in a Japanese naturalistic garden. When buying plant materials, it is advisable, if possible, to confine your selection to the plants on this list. If your nurseryman, however, cannot find exactly the same variety as that listed here, but has a slightly different one of the same species or family, closely resembling the listed plant in habit and hardiness, there will be no harm in substituting the available plant for the unobtainable listed one. But before you buy, it is a good idea to get proper assurance from the nurseryman as to the plant's hardiness, as well as full information on its planting, care, and habit.

It should be noted also that the dates given here for blossoming and fruiting are based on a climate equivalent to southern New England, southern New York State, and northern New Jersey. In areas north of this general region, where winters are longer and

Plate 240. Japanese Maple.
(See plant No. 10.)

Plate 241. Asian Serviceberry.
(See plant No. 15.)

Plate 242. Sasanqua Camellia.
(See plant No. 35.)

Plate 243. Deodar Cedar.
(See plant No. 37.)

Plate 244. American Bitter-sweet.
(See plant No. 39.)

colder, blossoming will occur two to four weeks later. depending, of course, upon how far north it is situated. Likewise, in those areas south of the southern New England region, where winters are shorter and warmer, blossoms will appear one to six weeks earlier, depending upon the latitude and elevation of the locality.

The plants are listed alphabetically by their scientific names, followed by their common English names and Japanese names. The common English and Japanese names are also included in the general index at the end of the book so that a reference can be found readily even when the scientific name is not known.

The following information, where applicable, is given for each of the plants listed. The information is given in the order shown here and employing the abbreviation indicated:

1. Scientific name, common English name, Japanese name.

2. Type of plant, e.g., whether tree, shrub, etc., and whether EVGR. (evergreen) or DEC. (deciduous).

3. The low Fahrenheit temperature hardiness of the plant. These are average and approximate figures. The actual critical low temperature for a given plant may vary as much as ten degrees lower or higher than the average temperature shown.

4. The type of environment required by the plant for optimum growth.

5. A brief description of the plant, including the average maximum height, in feet and/or inches, which the plant reaches. (Regular pruning and shearing will naturally keep the plant at much lower levels.)

6. A brief description of the plant's FL. (flowers) and/or FR. (fruit).

7. A final note upon the plant's special uses and characteristics. A plant designated DIO. (dioecious) has separate male and female varieties and both sexes must be planted together if fruit is desired.

1. *Abelia grandiflora*; Glossy Abelia. Dec. shrub. −8°. Sun, light shade, moist soil. Low, dense, 5′; glossy leaf, turns bronze purple autumn. Pink fl. Aug. thru mid-Oct. Hedge. Prune off dead twigs early spring. Hybrid.

2. *Abies concolor*; White Fir. Evgr. tree. −30°. Sun, moist soil. Medium height; dense silvery needles. Generally hardy; wind screen, hedge.

3. *A. firma*; Momi Fir; *momi*. Evgr. tree. −8°. Sunshine. Dense. stiff, pyramidal, horizontal branching.

4. *A. homolepis*; Nikko Fir. Evgr. tree. −15°. Sun, moist soil. Small tree, dark green needles. Hardy for city & roof garden; screen, hedge.

5. *A. koreana*; Korean Fir. Evgr. tree. −15°. Sun, moist soil. Medium height, green needles. Generally hardy; wind screen.

6. *A. nordmanniana*; Nordmann Fir. Evgr. tree. −15°. Sun, moist soil. Compact, large, Glossy green needles. Generally hardy; wind screen.

7. *A. veitchi*; Veitch Fir. Evgr. tree. −15°. Sun, moist soil. Compact, cone shaped, Needles. Generally hardy, Wind screen.

8. *Acanthopanax sieboldianus*; Acanthopa nax; *ukogi*. Dec. shrub. −15°. Shade: dry, sandy soil. 9′; dense, spreading, thorny. City hardy; holds leaves till late autumn.

9. *Acer ginnala*; Amur Maple. Dec. tree. −40°. Sun, light shade; dry, sandy soil. 20′; dense, spreading; small long green leaves. Bright red wings summer. Very hardy; scarlet leaves autumn.

10. *A. palmatum*; Japanese Maple; *momiji, kaede*. Dec. tree. −8°. Sun, light shade, moist soil. 20′, low, spreading, slow; green to red palmate lobed leaves. City hardy; scarlet leaves autumn. (See Plate 240.)

11. *A. rubrum*; Red Maple. Dec. tree. −15°. Sun, rich. moist soil. 75′; dense, compact, fast; early spring leaves. Red. fl. and

Plate 245. Katsura Tree.
(See plant No. 41.)

Plate 246. Flowering Quince.
(See plant No. 45.)

Plate 247. Hinoki Cypress.
(See plant No. 46.)

Plate 248. Sawara False Cypress.
(See plant No. 53.)

fr. early spring. Bright yellow & scarlet leaves autumn.

12. *A. saccharum;* Sugar Maple. Dec. tree. −25°. Dense, oval shape. Sugar made from sap. Bright orange, yellow, red leaves autumn.

13. *Actinidia arguta;* Bower Actinidia. Dec. vine. −15°. Sun or light shade; moist, good soil. 30'; climbing, twining, vigorous; dense, glossy leaves at end of red petioles; edible fr.; dio.

14. *Akebia quinata;* Five-leaf Akebia; *akebi.* Dec. vine. −15°. Sun, light shade, moist soil. 35'; vigorous, fast; green, thick leaves. Small purple fl.; long, purple, fleshy pods. City hardy; ground cover, fence, wall, bank.

15. *Amelanchier asiatica;* Asian Serviceberry, June Berry, Shadbush. Dec. small tree and shrub. −10°. Slender, spreading branches; 40'. White tomentose fl. on dense, nodding racemes in May. Fr. are dark berries in Sept. Does best in porous soil with moderate moisture, but hardy even in dry climates. (See Plate 241.)

16. *Arundinaria graminea (Pleioblastus);* bamboo grass variety; *taimin-chiku.* Evgr. grass. 0°. Sun, light shade; moist, good soil. 4–15'; low growing; grassy leaves. Ground cover; becomes deciduous in extreme cold; spreads by rhizomes.

17. *A. simoni (Pleioblastus);* Simon Bamboo; *kawa-take.* Evgr. grass. 8°. Sun, light shade; moist, good soil. 8'; dense; grows in clumps. Ground cover.

18. *Ardisia crispa (crenulata);* Coral Ardisia; *manryo.* Evgr. shrub. 25°. Deep shade; moist, good soil. 1'. Leathery, green leaves. White fl. spring and bright red berries autumn & winter.

19. *Artemisia frigida;* Fringed Sage Brush. Dec. shrub. −40°. Sun; dry, sandy soil. 1½'; silvery, pubescent, fine leaves. Small yellow fl. late August. Rock planting; aromatic foliage.

20. *Asarum asaroides (nipponicum, canadense, caudatum, virginicum);* Wild Ginger; *kanaoi.* Dec. herb. Needs shade, humus, moisture. Perennial, low growing. Interesting heart & kidney-shaped leaves; aromatic root stock. Used in rock planting.

21. *Aspidistra elatior;* Cast Iron Plant; *baran.* Evgr. herb. Hardy in intense heat, poor soil, dim light, & dust. Perennial; stiff, glossy leaves. Interesting design qualities.

22. *Aucuba japonica;* Japanese Aucuba; *aoki.* Evgr. shrub. 8°. Deep shade, moist soil. 15'; vigorous, spreading; glossy, thick leaves. Small panicled fl. & bright red berries. Dio.; leaves may have white or yellow spots.

23. *Berberis candidula;* Paleleaf Barberry. Evgr. shrub. −8°. Sun, light shade, moist soil. 2'; dwarf, dense; thorny twigs. Bright yellow fl. May; purple berries autumn. Hedge; rock planting.

24. *B. circumserrata;* Cutleaf Barberry. Dec. shrub. 8°. Sun, light shade, moist soil. 6'; dense rounded green leaf; thorny. Yellow fl. late May; yellow-red berry in autumn. Hardy; autumn leaves fiery red; hedge.

25. *B. koreana;* Korean Barberry. Dec. shrub. −8°. Sun, light shade, moist soil. 6'; dense, green leaves. Yellow, pendulous fl. clusters mid-May; bright red berry autumn and winter. Hedge, screen; leaves deep red autumn.

26. *B. mentorensis;* Mentor Barberry. Semi-evgr. shrub. −15°. Hardy in hot, dry, poor soil. 7'; dense, spiny, green leaves; thorny. Yellow fl. May, dark red berries autumn. Hedge, screen; hybrid; hardy in cold winter & hot dry summer.

27. *B. thunbergi;* Japanese Barberry. Dec. shrub. −8°. Hardy in any soil; hot, dry area. 7'; dense, low green leaves, changing to scarlet in autumn. Yellow-red in mid-May, bright red berry in autumn & winter. Hedge; bank; ground cover; thorny; city and seashore hardy.

28. *Betula lenta;* Sweet Birch. Dec. tree. −25°. 70'; dense foliage. Bark & twigs aromatic taste. Yellow leaves autumn; reddish brown bark. (DON'T PRUNE BIRCHES IN SPRING.)

29. *B. lutea;* Yellow Birch. Dec. tree. −25°. Sun, light shade; hardy in moist, dry soil. Grows in clumps; light green leaves. Golden yellow bark; yellow leaves autumn. Withstands much pruning.

30. *B. papyrifera;* Paper or White Birch. Dec. tree. −40°. Sun, light shade; hardy in poor soil. Tall, single white trunk, light green leaves. Best in moist soil; yellow leaves autumn.

31. *B. populifolia;* American Gray Birch; *shira-kaba.* Dec. tree. −25°. Sun, light shade; hardy in poor sandy soil. Grows in clumps; light green leaves; light gray bark. Hardy; does well near seashore; yellow leaves autumn.

32. *Buxus microphylla (japonica, compacta, koreana);* Little-leaf Box (Japanese, Korean); *tsuge.* Evgr. shrub. −8°. Sun or light shade; moist soil. Compact, low, slow growing, 4', dense. Korean variety most hardy; withstands low temperature; hedge, screen.

33. *Callicarpa japonica;* Japanese Beautyberry; *murasaki-shikibu.* Dec. shrub. −8°. 4'; upright. Pink & white fl. early June; purple berries autumn. Prune early spring for vigorous growth.

34. *Camellia japonica;* Common Camellia; *yama-tsubaki.* Evgr. shrub/tree. 10°. Best in shade. 40'; dark, lustrous, green, leathery leaves. White to red single or double fl. Oct. to Apr. Grows best N. Carolina, South, Gulf Coast, Pacific Coast. Screen.

35. *C. sasanqua;* Sasanqua Camellia; *sazanka.* Evgr. tree/shrub. 10°. Best in shade. 20'; leaves dark green, lustrous; open, loose. White to pink fl. Sept. to Dec. Hedge, screen; fragrant flowers. (See Plate 242.)

36. *Campsis grandiflora (chinensis);* Chinese Trumpet Creeper; *nozen-kazura.* Dec. vine. 10°. 20'; clinging. Scarlet funnel-shape fl. Aug.

37. *Cedrus deodara;* Deodar Cedar; *himaraya-sugi.* Evgr. tree. 0°. Sun; moist good soil. Tall, elegant, bluish, green needles. Best in Pacific-coast NW and in mid-Atlantic states. (See Plate 243.)

38. *Celastrus orbiculata;* Oriental Bittersweet; *tsuru-ume-modoki.* Dec. vine. −15°. 36'; round leaves; turn yellow autumn. Red

Plate 249. Thread Sawara False Cypress.
(See plant No. 54.)

Plate 250. Golden Thread Sawara False Cypress.
(See plant No. 54.)

Plate 251. Moss Sawara False Cypress.
(See plant No. 56.)

Plate 252. Spike Winter-hazel.
(See plant No. 67.)

Plate 253. American Smoke Tree.
(See plant No. 68.)

& yellow berries autumn & winter. Dio.; twining habit.

39. *C. scandens;* American Bittersweet. Dec. vine. −40°. Grows well in shade. 20′; rampant, shrubby, twining; yellow leaves autumn. Red & yellow berries autumn & winter. Dio.; excellent in bank planting; hardy at seashore. (See Plate 244.)

40. *Cephalotaxus drupacea;* Chinese Plum Yew; *chosen-maki.* Evgr. shrub. −15°. Hardy in sheltered spots. 30′; shrubby, slow growing. Reddish brown, plume-like fruit.

41. *Cercidiphyllum japonicum;* Katsura Tree; *katsura.* Dec. tree. −8°. Sun or light shade; rich, moist soil. 30′; round light green leaves changing to purple & yellow. Scarlet leaves autumn; hardy from Mass. southwards. (See Plate 245.)

42. *Cercis canadensis;* Eastern Redbud, Judas Tree. Dec. tree. −15°. Shade, moist, good soil. 40′. Pink fl. May. Yellow leaves autumn.

43. *C. chinensis;* Chinese Judas Tree; *hana-zuo.* Dec. tree. 0°. 40′. Rosy purple fl. dense mid-May. Yellow leaves autumn; shrubby habit in North.

44. *Chaenomeles japonica;* Japanese Quince. Dec. shrub. −15°. Good soil; moderate moisture. 3′; low, dense; thorny. Single red fl. early May. Green, apple-like fr. changing to yellow. Hardy in city; little pruning.

45. *C. lagenaria;* Flowering Quince; *boke, karin.* Dec. shrub. −15°. Any good, moist soil. 6′; dark green, shiny leaves; dense, thorny. White to dark red, single, double fl. early May and green apple-like fr. Also hardy in dry, sandy soil. Hedge. (See Plate 246.)

46. *Chamaecyparis obtusa;* Hinoki Cypress; *hinoki.* Evgr. shrub/tree. −25°. Sun or light shade; moderate moisture. Scale-like foliage. Slow growing. (See Plate 247.)

47. *C. o. compacta;* Compact Hinoki Cypress. Evgr. shrub. −25°. Sun or light shade; moderate moisture. Dwarf, broad, conical.

48. *C. o. filicoides;* Fernspray Hinoki Cypress. Evgr. shrub. −25°. Sun or light shade; moderate moisture. Lateral branchlets of equal length, fernlike.

49. *C. o. gracilis;* Slender Hinoki Cypress. Evgr. shrub. −25°. Sun or light shade; moderate moisture. 8′.

50. *C. o. lycopodioides;* Clubmoss Hinoki Cypress. Evgr. shrub. −25°. Sun or light shade; moderate moisture. Dwarf, shrubby. Branchlets in one plane.

51. *C. o. pygmaea;* Pygmy Hinoki Cypress. Evgr. shrub. −25°. Sun or light shade; moderate moisture. Creeping prostrate branches. Grows slowly.

52. *C. o. pendula;* Weeping Hinoki Cypress; *suiryu-hiba.* Evgr. shrub. −25°. Sun or light shade; moderate moisture. Hedges & foundation planting.

53. *C. pisifera;* Sawara False Cypress; *sawara.* Evgr. shrub/tree. −25°. Sun or light shade. Makes good dense hedge. Hardy in city, roof gardens, seashore; periodic shearing & pruning necessary to control growth & increase density & compactness. (See Plate 248.)

54. *C. p. filifera;* Thread Sawara False Cypress. Evgr. shrub/tree. −25°. Pyramidal; threadlike branchlets. Hardy in city, roof gardens, seashore; periodic shearing & pruning necessary to control growth & increase density & compactness. Also *aurea,* Golden variety. (See Plates 249–50.)

55. *C. p. minima;* Midget Sawara False Cypress. Low, shrubby short branches.

56. *C. p. squarrosa;* Moss Sawara False Cypress; *himuro.* Frondlike soft foliage. Grayish blue; bronze in autumn. (See Plate 251.)

57. *Chimonanthus praecox;* Winter-sweet; *robai.* Dec. shrub. 8°. Light shade. 8′. Yellow, purplish, brown, striped fl. April. Fragrant; needs little pruning.

58. *Clematis montana rubens;* Pink Anemone Clematis. Dec. vine. 8°. Best in sun. 24′; new leaves bronze/crimson. Red to pink fl. May; plumy seed heads summer. Flower buds on previous year's wood; screen.

59. *C. paniculata;* Sweet Autumn Clematis. Semi-evgr. vine. −8°. Best in sun, 30′; lustrous, green leaves. White, fragrant, profuse fl. late Aug.; plumy, silvery seed heads. Garden screen, hedge, bank; city hardy.

60. *Clerodendron trichotomum;* Harlequin Glory-bower. Dec. shrub. 0°. 20′; horizontal branches from single stem. White, slightly fragrant fl. Aug.; blue berries in bright red calyx. Red calyx remains long after berries drop.

61. *Clethra barbinervis;* Japanese Clethra; *ryobu.* Dec. shrub. −8°. Acid soil. 30′. White fl. late July. Plant resistant to red spider.

62. *Cornus alba sibirica;* Siberian Dogwood. Dec. shrub/tree. −15°. Moist, fertile soil; 9′; winter twigs bright coral red; red leaves autumn. Yellow-white, small fl. late May; blue-white berries autumn. City hardy; must prune rigorously early spring.

63. *Cornus florida;* White Flowering Dogwood; *yama-boshi.* Dec. shrub tree. −15°. Sun or shade; moist, fertile soil. 20′; picturesque crown; red leaves autumn. White fl. May. Scarlet berries Aug.-Oct. Native American variety.

64. *Cornus kousa;* Japanese Dogwood; *yama-momiji.* Dec. shrub/tree. −15°. Moist, fertile soil; best in light shade. 20′; fan shaped, irregular branches. Creamy white fl. June-July; pink fr. Aug.-Sept. Brilliant red leaves autumn; ideal foundation planting, walls.

65. *Cornus officinalis;* Japanese Cornel; *sanshuyu.* Dec. tree. −8°. Sun or light shade; moist, good soil. 30′; shiny green leaves; dense. Small, yellow fl. early Apr.; scarlet edible fr. Aug. Red leaves in autumn; bark exfoliates in winter.

66. *Corylopsis glabrescens;* Fragrant Winter-hazel. Dec. shrub. −8°. Shade. 18′; flat, rounded crown, dense leaves. Pale yellow fl. mid-Apr.

67. *Corylopsis spicata;* Spike Winter-hazel. Dec. shrub. 0°. Low habit. Bright yellow, fragrant fl. in spikes early spring. Handsome foliage. Prefers peaty, sandy soil. (See Plate 252.)

Plate 254. Nippon Hawthorn.
(See plant No. 71.)

Plate 255. China Fir.
(See plant No. 74.)

Plate 256. Monterey Cypress.
(See plant No. 75.)

Plate 257. Hooker's St. Johnswort.
(See plant No. 101.)

Plate 258. Japanese Holly.
(See plant No. 103.)

68. *Cotinus americanus;* American Smoke Tree. Dec. tree. −8°. 25'; upright; dense leaves. Feathery mass of fine textured fl. From a distance fl. look like smoke. Scarlet autumn leaves. (See Plate 253.)

69. *Cotoneaster horizontalis;* Rockspray. Semi-evgr. shrub. −15°. Sun; moist soil. 3'; horizontal, low branching habit. Small pink fl. mid-June; bright red berries early autumn. Periodic shearing necessary; ground cover, banks; seashore hardy.

70. *C. racemiflora sungarica;* Sungari Rockspray. Dec. shrub. −25°. Moist soil. 7'; grayish-green, rounded leaves. Small white fl. early June; profuse pink berries autumn. Hardy at seashore.

71. *Crataegus cuneata;* Nippon Hawthorn; *sanzashi.* Dec. shrub. −15°. White, pink, red fl.; red berries autumn. City hardy; withstands heavy pruning; hedges. (See Plate 254.)

72. *C. phaenopyrum;* Washington Hawthorn Dec. tree. −15°. 25'; upright; dense, twiggy, thorny. White fl. mid-June; bright red berries all winter. Scarlet autumn leaves.

73. *Cryptomeria japonica;* Cryptomeria; *sugi.* Evgr. tree. −15°. Best in sun, clean, clear air. 18–85'; tall, narrow, scale-like leaves. Winter tips get brownish; withstands heavy pruning; not hardy in city.

74. *Cunninghamia lanceolata (chinensis);* Common China Fir; *koyozan.* Evgr. tree. 10°. Moist soil. 65'; needles; spreading, slightly drooping branches. When cut down, sprouts from stump & roots. Good in areas of mild winters. (See Plate 255.)

75. *Cupressus macrocarpa;* Monterey Cypress; *seiyo-hinoki.* Evgr. tree. 8°. Moist soil. 65'; broad and rounded as it grows old. Used in clipped hedges & at seashore; in areas of mild winters. (See Plate 256.)

76. *Cycas revoluta;* Sago Cycas; *sotetsu.* Evgr. shrub. 20°. Sun; moist fertile soil. 10'; dark, shiny, fernlike leaves; slow growing. Trunk looks like a pineapple or a palm tree.

77. *Cytisus scoparius;* Scotch Broom; *enishida.* Dec. shrub. −8°. Sun; acid, sandy, dry soil. 6'; bushy. Yellow, pea-like fl. mid-May. Green twigs winter; hardy at seashore.

78. *Daphne odora;* Winter Daphne; *jinchoge.* Evgr. shrub. 8°. Light shade; moist, cool root condition. 4–6'. Small, rose-purple, fragrant fl. Mar.-Apr. Should not prune, cultivate, or fertilize.

79. *Deutzia gracilis;* Slender Deutzia. Dec. shrub. −15°. 5'; dense, compact, arching branches. Profuse white fl. late May.

80. *Elaeagnus multiflora;* Cherry Elaeagnus. Dec. shrub. −15°. 9'; dark green leaves, silvery underside. Yellow, white, fragrant fl. mid-May; red, scaly, edible acidy berries. Thorny stems; hardy near seashore.

81. *Enkianthus campanulatus;* Red-vein Enkianthus; *sarasadodan.* Dec. shrub. −15°. Light shade; moist, acid soil. 15'; compact form. Yellow, orange, bell-shaped, pendulous clusters mid-May. Autumn leaves bright red & orange.

82. *E. perulatus;* White Enkianthus; *dodantsutsuji.* Dec. shrub. −8°. Light shade; acid moist soil. 6'; neat. White bell-shaped fl. early May. Autumn leaves bright scarlet.

83. *Equisetum hyemale;* Horse Tail, Scouring Rush; *tokusa.* Evgr. herb. 8°. Moist, sandy soil. 3'; low, spine-like perennial. Related to ferns; has spores in conelike spikes. Hollow, jointed stems; used in shoreline planting and along streams.

84. *Euonymus alata compacta;* Winged Spindle Tree; *komayumi.* Dec. shrub −25°. 9'; dwarf, compact, dense; lateral branching habit. Scarlet fr. autumn. Hardy in city; leaves scarlet autumn; corky ridges on twigs; hedges.

85. *E. japonica;* Evergreen Euonymus; *masaki.* Evgr. shrub. 15°. Hardy in dry, sandy soil. 15'; dense; profuse, lustrous leaves. Pinkish orange fr. autumn. City & seashore hardy; hedges.

86. *E. yedoensis;* Yedo Euonymus. Dec. shrub. −15°. 15'; flat topped; bright red leaves autumn. Pink to purple fr. autumn. City hardy.

87. *E. fortunei vegeta;* Winter Creeper. Evgr. shrub/vine. −8°. Sun or light shade. Compact; small leathery leaves. Colorful fruit autumn. Can be trained as vine, ground cover; clings to walls, fences, rocks, trees.

88. *Eurya japonica;* Japanese Eurya; *hisakaki.* Evgr. shrub. 8°. Moist soil. Greenish white fl.; black berries autumn. Dense foliage. 20'. Used in hedges.

89. *Fatsia japonica;* Japanese Fatsia; *yatsude.* Evgr. shrub. 8°. Best in shade; hardy in poor soil. 15'; long, leathery, shiny, lobed leaves. White fl. on large panicles autumn; light blue berries winter. Needs little care; hardy at seashore & city.

90. *Ficus carica;* Fig; *ichijiku.* Dec. shrub. 0°. 15–25'; large leaves. Purple, edible fr. autumn.

91. *Forsythia ovata;* Early Forsythia. Dec. shrub. −15°. Sun or light shade; moist soil. 8'. Small yellow fl. early Apr. Earliest to bloom; hardiest even in city gardens.

92. *F. suspensa sieboldi;* Siebold Forsythia; *rengyo.* Dec. shrub. −8°. Sun or light shade; hardy in moist, poor soil. 5–10'; drooping, trailing habit. Bright yellow fl. mid-Apr. Hardy in city & in roof gardens. Should be pruned after blooming.

93. *Gardenia jasminoides;* Cape Jasmine or Gardenia; *kuchi-nashi.* Evgr. shrub. 20°. Shade; moist soil. 5'; thick, leathery, shiny leaves. Waxy white fragrant fl. May to Sept.

94. *Gaultheria miqueliana;* Miquel Wintergreen. Evgr. shrub. −8°. 1'. White fl. May; pinkish white berries autumn.

95. *Gingko biloba;* Gingko, Maiden-hair Tree; *icho.* Dec. tree. −15°. Sun; hardy in poor soil. 50'; leathery, fan-shaped leaves. Male tree preferred; female fruit smell bad. Bright yellow leaves autumn. Very hardy; resists smoke, dust, drought, adverse city conditions. Dio.

96. *Hamamelis mollis;* Chinese Witch-hazel. Dec. shrub. −8°. Does well in shade. 30'; bright yellow leaves autumn. Yellow fragrant fl. with ribbon-like petals March. Hardy in city.

Plate 259. Pfitzer Juniper.
(See plant No. 108.)

Plate 260. Sargent Juniper.
(See plant No. 109.)

Plate 261. Beauty Bush.
(See plant No. 116.)

Plate 262. Maackia.
(See plant No. 132.)

Plate 263. Leatherleaf Mahonia.
(See plant No. 135.)

97. *Hibiscus rosa-sinensis;* Chinese Hibiscus; *bussoge.* Dec. shrub. 25°. 30'; fast growing, glossy leaves. White, pink, red fl. summer. City hardy; for warm winter areas; hedge.

98. *H. syriacus;* Rose of Sharon, Shrub Althea; *mukuge.* Dec. shrub. −8°. Normal garden soil. 15'; dense, bushy. Large white to blue fl. Aug. City and seashore hardy; hedges.

99. *Hydrangea macrophylla hortensia;* House Hydrangea; *ajisai.* Dec. shrub. 0°. 12'; bright green, shiny leaves. Acid soil makes blue fl.; alkaline, pink fl. in Aug. Not so hardy in north, but city and seashore hardy. Hedges.

100. *H. paniculata grandiflora;* Peegee Hydrangea. Dec. shrub. −15°. 25'; large coarse leaves. White clustered fl. Aug. City hardy.

101. *Hypericum hookerianum;* Hooker's St. Johnswort. Evgr. to semi-evgr. shrub. 10°. Compact habit; 6'. Reddish brown branches; large, cup-shaped, yellow fl. in profusion blooming in Aug. Prefers good, loamy soils, moisture and partial shade. (See Plate 257.)

102. *Hypericum patulum henryi;* Henry St. Johnswort; *kinshibai.* Semi-evgr. shrub. 0°. 3'. Yellow fl. July. Hedges.

103. *Ilex crenata;* Japanese Holly; *kikkotsuge, inutsuge* Evgr. shrub. 0°. Shade, acid soil. 15'; lustrous, dark green leaves. Small black berries autumn. Dio.; hardy in city & in roof gardens; dense hedges.

104. *I. pedunculosa;* Long-stalk Holly; *soyogo.* Evgr. shrub. −8°. Shade, acid soil, 30'; lustrous, dark green leaves. Bright red berries autumn. Dio.; hardy in any environment. (See Plate 258.)

105. *I. verticillata;* Black Alder, Winterberry. Dec. shrub. −25°. Sun or light shade; moist, acid soil. 9'. Bright red berries autumn & winter. Dio.; thrives near seashore; hedges.

106. *Indigofera kirilowi;* Kirilow Indigo. Dec. shrub. −15°. Withstands sandy, dry soil. 3'; low, dense. Small rose-colored spiked fl. June. Spreads fast by underground rhizomes. Ground cover.

107. *Jasminum nudiflorum;* Winter Jasmine; *obai.* Dec. vine. −8°. Dry, sun area. 15'; graceful, drooping; green twigs in winter. Bright yellow fl. early Apr. By walls and banks; blooms in winter in South. Requires pruning.

108. *Juniperus chinensis pfitzeriana;* Pfitzer Juniper; *byakushin, ibuki, kaizukaibuki.* Evgr. shrub. −15°. Sun; sandy, dry, poor, alkaline soil. 10'; broad, flat-top, feathery needles. Blue berries autumn. City, seashore hardy. Roof gardens, hedges; grows close to ground. (See Plate 259.)

109. *J. chinensis sargenti;* Sargent Juniper. Evgr. shrub. −15°. Dry, sunny, sandy, alkaline soil. Low prostrate, creeping; steel blue needles. Blue berries autumn. Dio.; ground cover in banks; fragrant needles; seashore hardy. (See Plate 260.)

110. *J. converta;* Shore Juniper; *hainezu.* Evgr. shrub. −8°. Dry, sandy, alkaline soil; sun. Low, creeping; fragrant needles. Dio.; hardy in sand-dunes; ground cover.

111. *J. horizontalis procumbens;* Flat Creeping Juniper; *haibyakushin.* Evgr. shrub. −40°. Sun; dry, alkaline soil. Blue-green fragrant needles. Blue berries autumn. Dio.; used on banks; ground cover.

112. *J. virginiana;* Eastern Red Cedar. Evgr. tree. −40°. Alkaline soil. 80'; dense, pyramidal, columnar. Small, round, blue berries autumn. Dio.; scalelike leaves.

113. *Kadsura japonica;* Scarlet Kadsura; *binan-kazura.* Evgr. vine. 8°. Twining; leaves turn red autumn. Yellowish white fl. June. to Sept. Scarlet berry clusters autumn. Ground cover, screen, fence, and wall cover.

114. *Kalmia latifolia;* Mountain Laurel. Evgr. shrub. −15°. Acid, moist soil; sun or light shade. 10'. Pink and white clustered fl. mid-June. City hardy.

115. *Kerria japonica;* Kerria; *yamabuki.* Dec. shrub. −15°. 5'; drooping, green branch all winter. Profuse yellow fl. May through June. City hardy; requires pruning.

116. *Kolkwitzia amabilis;* Beauty Bush. Dec. shrub. −15°. Hardy in dry, sandy areas. 10'; upright, arching, drooping; fast grow-

ing; red leaves autumn. Profuse, pink fl. early June; brown, bristly seeds. Bark exfoliates in winter. (See Plate 261.)

117. *Kraunhia floribunda;* Japanese Wisteria; *fuji.* Dec. vine. −15°. Blooms best in sun, but hardy in shade. 24'; fast; twining. Violet, blue, pendulous racemes, late fl. May. Hardy by seashore & city roof gardens.

118. *Lagerstroemia indica;* Crape Myrtle; *saru-suberi.* Dec. shrub. 8°. 21'; vigorous, rounded form. Profuse, bright, pink-red fl. Aug. Hardy as far north as Maryland; used in hedges, city hardy.

119. *Larix leptolepis;* Larch; *rakuyoso, karamatsu.* Dec. tree. −8°. Short, needle-shaped leaves in clusters. Hardy; cone bearing.

120. *Laurus nobilis;* Laurel, Sweet Bay; *gekkeiju.* Evgr. shrub. 0°. Best in shade; moist, humus, loamy soil. Long, aromatic leaves. Green-white fl. early June; dark green to black berries autumn. Withstands shearing, pruning.

121. *Leiophyllum buxifolium;* Box Sand-myrtle. Evgr. shrub. −8°. Acid, well-drained soil; light shade. 18"; low; tiny, glossy leaves turn brown in autumn. Small, waxy, white fl. May. Plant in clumps not singly; good ground cover.

122. *Lespedeza bicolor;* Shrub Bush-clover; *hagi.* Dec. shrub. −15°. Light, sandy, dry soil. 9'; perennial. Purple fl. late summer. May be heavily pruned.

123. *L. japonica;* Japanese Bush-clover. Dec. shrub. −8°. 6'. White fl. Oct.

124. *Leucothoe catesbaei;* Drooping Leucothoe. Evgr. to semi-evgr. −15°. Acid, moist, shaded area. 6'; lustrous, dark leaves turning bronze in autumn. White racemes, arching stems, early June. Used in banks; city hardy.

125. *L. keiskei;* Keisk's Leucothoe. Evgr. shrub. −8°. Acid, shaded soil. 4'; graceful, slender; leathery leaves. Pendulous, white fl. late May.

126. *Ligustrum japonicum;* Japanese Privet; *nezumi-mochi.* Evgr. shrub. 8°. Hardy in

Plate 264. Banana Shrub.
(See plant No. 140.)

Plate 265. Nandina.
(See plant No. 143.)

sun or shade. 10–20′; vigorous, fast. Small, white, clustered fl. mid-July; black berries autumn. City hardy; clipped hedges and screens.

127. *L. obtusifolium var. regelianum*; Border Privet (Regel). Dec. shrub. −25° Hardy in dry soil, sun or shade. 5–10′; low-lateral branching in habit; leaves turn brown-purple autumn. White fl. mid-June; blue, black berries. Very hardy in city; hedges.

128. *L. ovalifolium*; California Privet; *obaiibota*. Semi-evgr. shrub. −25°. Hardy in sun or shade. 15′; lustrous green leaves. Creamy white fl. mid-June, black berries. City hardy.

129. *Lonicera japonica halliana*; Hall's Japanese Honeysuckle. Semi-evgr. vine. −15°. Generally hardy any environment. Vigorous, twining; leaves turn bronze autumn. White-yellow, fragrant fl. early June; black berries autumn. Hardy near seashore, in city, roof gardens; used on trellis, banks, as ground cover.

130. *L. maacki*; Amur Honeysuckle. Dec. shrub. −40°. Best in sun, dry soil, but hardy in shade. 15′; leaves last till late autumn. White to yellow fragrant fl. late May; red berries Sept. through Nov. Generally hardy in city; used in hedges.

131. *L. morrowi*; Morrow Honeysuckle; *kingin-boku*. Dec. shrub. −15°. Best in sun, dry soil, but will do in shade. 6′; dense, moundlike, sprawling. White to yellow, fragrant fl. & red berries June through July. City and seashore hardy.

132. *Maackia floribunda*; Maackia. Dec. tree. −5°. 40′. Large, pinnate leaves; dense, upright panicles of small, white fl. blooming in July-Aug. Flat seed pods. Prefers warm, sunny locations. (See Plate 262.)

133. *Magnolia liliflora nigra*; Purple Lily Magnolia; *mokuren* or *shimokuren*. Dec. shrub. 0°. 10′. Purple fl. mid-May; red, pod-like fr. early fall. Has several trunks.

134. *M. stellata*; Star Magnolia; *shide-kobushi*. Dec. tree. −8°. Best in sun. 20′; dense habit; long leaves turning bronze in fall. Double, white fragrant fl. mid-Apr.; red,

pod-like fr. early fall. Hardiest of all magnolias; city hardy; grow in northern exposure to retard blooming in the North.

135. *Mahonia beali (japonica)*; Leatherleaf Mahonia; *hiragi-nanten*. Evgr. shrub. 0°. Prefers shady, sheltered location. 12′. Leathery, bluish-green, pinnate leaves. Yellow, fragrant fl. in racemes & panicles; dark blue berries. Do not expose to winter sun. (See Plate 263.)

136. *Malus floribunda*; Japanese Flowering Crab-apple. Dec. shrub-tree. −15°. 20′; picturesque, graceful branching. Pink fl. May, yellow to red fr. Hardy in city, seashore, and roof gardens.

137. *M. sieboldi*; Toringo Crab-apple. Dec. shrub tree. −15°. 20′; picturesque, graceful branching. Pink fl. May; yellow to red fr. Hardy in city, seashore, and roof gardens.

138. *M. sargenti*; Sargent Crab-apple. Dec. shrub. −8°. 6′; dense mounded form. White, fragrant fl. mid-May; dark red persistent fall fruit.

139. *M. toringoides*; Cutleaf Crab-apple. Dec. tree. −8°. 20′; upright, pyramidal, dense, branching. White fragrant fl. late May; yellow, red fr. Aug. through Nov. As in case of all apples, insect control required.

140. *Michelia fuscata*; Banana Shrub. Evgr. shrub. 10°. 15′. Yellow, white, maroon edged fl. spring. Best in areas of mild winters; flowers have odor of banana. (See Plate 264.)

141. *Miscanthus sinensis (japonicus)*; Eulalia, Chinese Silver Grass; *susuki*. Dec. grass. −20°. Any moist good soil. 4′ to 10′; silky, plumelike panicles. Graceful but sharp leaves; hardy in regions of cold winters.

142. *Myrica pennsylvania*; Bayberry. Semi-evgr. shrub. −40°. Acid, wet, sandy, and shady. 9′; aromatic leaves. Waxy, gray berries fall to winter. Dio.: hardy at seashore & in city.

143. *Nandina domestica*; Nandina; *nanten*. Evgr. shrub. 8°. 8′; spring leaves pink to bronze. White fl. late July; bright red berries autumn through winter. Autumn foliage red to scarlet. (See Plate 265.)

144. *Nerium oleander*; Oleander. Evgr. shrub. 15°. Hardy in hot, dry places; sandy soil. 20′; bamboo-like. White, red, yellow, purple fl. Apr. through Sept. In southern gardens: control by root pruning; used in hedges.

145. *Osmanthus fortunei*; Fortune Osmanthus. Evgr. shrub. 15°. Light shade. 12′; shiny, hollylike leaves. Yellow, fragrant fl. June; blue-black berries autumn. Hybrid; vigorous, growing in South and on Pacific Coast.

146. *Osmanthus fragrans*; Fragrant Osmanthus; *moukusei, ginmokusei, kinmokusei*. Evgr. shrub. 20°. Large, lanceolate, coriaceous leaves; small, white, fragrant fl. in axillary clusters blooming in early spring. 10′. Also another variety: *Osmanthus fragrans aurantiacus*; Golden Osmanthus; *Kinmokusei*. (See Plate 266.)

147. *O. ilicifolius*; Holly Osmanthus; *hiiragi*. Evgr. shrub. 0°. Sun or light shade. 18′; glossy green leaves; spiny. Greenish yellow fragrant fl. July; blue-black berries autumn. Clipped hedge. (See Plate 267.)

148. *Pachysandra terminalis*; Japanese Spurge or Pachysandra. Evgr. herb. −10°. Light shade. Ground cover; dark green glossy leaves. Small white spiked fl. early May; white berries autumn. Hardy in city, roof gardens, banks; uniform height in bed.

149. *Paeonia suffruticosa*; Tree Peony; *botan*. Dec. shrub. −10°. Rich, well drained, alkaline soil. 5′. White, rose-red; single, double fl.

150. *Parthenocissus tricuspidata*; Boston Ivy; *tsuta (thunbergi)*. Dec. vine. −15°. Clinging vine; lustrous leaves turning red autumn. Blue-black berries autumn. Clings to stonework; city hardy.

151. *P. quinquefolia*; Virginia Creeper, Woodbine. Dec. vine. −25°. Partial shade. High climbing vine; leaves turn red in fall. Blue-black berries in autumn. Clings by tendrils; city hardy; used in banks.

152. *Philadelphus purpurascens*; Purple Cup, Mock Orange. Dec. shrub. −8°. Good soil. 12′; dense. White, fragrant, purple

Plate 266. Golden Osmanthus.
(See plant No. 146.)

Plate 267. Holly Osmanthus.
(See plant No. 147.)

Plate 268. Tanyosho Pine.
(See plant No. 160.)

Plate 269. Japanese White Pine.
(See plant No. 163.)

Plate 270. Shrubby Yew Podocarpus.
(See plant No. 167.)

calyxed fl. mid-June. Used as screen; withstands much pruning.

153. *Photinia glabra*; Japanese Photinia; *kanamemochi*. Semi-evgr. shrub. 0°. Moist soil. 15'; elliptical, fine-toothed leaves. White panicled fl. & red fr. May through July. Red to scarlet leaves. Excellent in sheared hedges.

154. *P. serrulata*; Chinese Photinia. Evgr. shrub. 8°. Well-drained soil. 36'; dark lustrous green leaves. White fl. mid-May; red berries fall through early winter. Spring foliage brilliant reddish bronze.

155. *P. villosa*; Oriental Photinia. Dec. shrub. −15°. 15'; dark green, glabrous leaves. Small, white fl. late May; red berries autumn. Autumn leaves red to bronze.

156. *Phyllostachys aurea*; Golden Bamboo. Evgr. 10°. Moist soil. 30'; grows in clumps; spreads slowly.

157. *P. bambusoides*; Timber Bamboo. Evgr. 15°. Moist soil. 50'; open growing; feathery leaves. Edible sprouts.

158. *Picea polita*; Tigertail Spruce; *tohi*. Evgr. tree. −5°. Best in sun. 60'; stiff needles. Pyramidal habit.

159. *Pieris japonica*; Japanese Andromeda; *asebi*. Evgr. shrub. −8°. Best in sun. 9'; lustrous, dark green broad-leaf. White, pendulous, clustered fl. mid-Apl. Low habit; spring leaves rich bronze; needs winter protection in New England; city hardy.

160. *Pinus densiflora umbraculifera*; Tanyo-sho Pine. Evgr. tree. −15°. Best in sunny areas. 12', flat-topped habit. Yellowish green needles in winter. (See Plate 268.)

161. *P. koraiensis*; Korean Pine; *chosen-goyo, chosen-matsu*. Evgr. tree. −25°. Moist, sandy, well drained soil; sun. 80'; pyramidal, compact, dense. Long cones. Dark green needles; slow growing; good in small gardens.

162. *P. mugo mughus*; Mugo Pine. Evgr. shrub-tree. −40°. Hardy in poor, sandy soil. 8'; dwarf, compact, shrubby. Hardy in windy areas such as seashore.

163. *P. parviflora*; Japanese White Pine; *goyo-matsu*. Evgr. tree. −8°. Sunshine; moist, well drained soil. 80'; low, wide-spreading branches. needles in dense, small tufts. (See Plate 269.)

164. *P. strobus* (varieties); Eastern White Pine. Evgr. tree. −25°. Sunny; poor, sandy soil. 30'; fast growing. Older trees lose lower branches.

165. *P. thunbergi*; Japanese Black Pine; *kuro-matsu*. Evgr. tree. −15°. Sunny places. 50'; irregular, picturesque branching. Hardy by seashore.

166. *Pittisporum tobira*; Japanese Pittis-porum; *tobera*. Evgr. shrub. 15°. Partial shade; hardy in dry, sandy soil 10'; dark green, lustrous, leathery leaves. White fragrant fl. May. Seashore and city hardy; used in hedges; common in deep South.

167. *Podocarpus macrophyllus (macro-phylla)*; Shrubby Yew Podocarpus; *inu-maki*. Evgr. tree. 8°. Sunshine; moist, sandy, humus loam. 50'; horizontal, pendulous branching; dense; lance-shaped leaves. Used extensively in sheared hedges and alone; needs mild winters. (See Plate 270.)

168. *Prunus glandulosa*; Dwarf Flowering Almond. Dec. shrub. −15°. 5'. Pink, white fl. early May; red cherries in summer.

169. *P. higanzakura*; Japanese Flowering Cherry. *kizo-zakura*. Dec. tree. −15°. 30'. Pink fl. Apr. Seashore & city hardy.

170. *P. japonica nakai*; Nakai Chinese Bush Cherry. Dec. shrub. −40°. 4–5'. Pink-white fl. early May; and red cherries summer.

171. *P. kanzan*; Japanese Flowering Cherry; *kanzan-zakura*. Dec. tree. −15°. 30'. Large, dark pink fl. Apr. Seashore & city hardy.

172. *P. maritima*; Beach Plum. Dec. shrub/tree. −25°. Dry, sandy places. 15'; dense rounded habit. White fl. early May; purple plums late summer. Seashore hardy; picturesque branching habit.

173. *P. nipponica*; Nippon Cherry. Dec. Tree. −8°. 15'; dense, bushy. Single, white

to pale pink fl. late Apr. Yellow, orange crimson leaves autumn.

174. *P. sargenti*; Sargent Cherry. Dec. tree. −15°. 65'; upright; round top. Pink, single fl. late Apr. Red leaves autumn.

175. *P. serrulata alba plena*; Double Chinese Flowering Cherry; *sato-zakura*. Dec. tree. −15°. 30'. White, double fl. Apr. Seashore & city hardy.

176. *P. shirofugen*; Victory Flowering Cherry. Dec. tree. −15°. 30' high. White fl. Apr. Seashore & city hardy.

177. *P. subhirtella pendula*; Weeping Higan Cherry; *shidare-zakura*. Dec. tree. −15°. 30'; pendulous branches. Pink fl. Apr. Seashore & city hardy.

178. *P. tomentosa*; Manchu Cherry; *yusura-ume*. Dec. shrub. −40°. 9'. Pinkish white fl. late Apr.; red cherries June through July. Often used in flowering hedge.

179. *Pseudosasa japonica*; Metake or Arrow Bamboo. Evgr. 0°. 10–20'. Spreads slowly by rhizomes; height depends upon winter temperatures.

180. *Pseudotsuga taxifolia douglasi*; Douglas Fir. Evgr. tree. 10°. Grows high in compact pyramidal form.

181. *Punica granatum*; Pomegranate; *zakuro*. Dec. tree. 10°. Needs winter protection. 15' high. Scarlet to pink fl. summer; red-yellow fr. autumn. Fruit edible; hardy in dry sandy places.

182. *Pyracantha coccinea (lalandi)*; Scarlet (Laland) Firethorn. Dec. in North, evgr. in South. 0°. Partial shade. 6'; spiny, thorny, dense, vigorous. Small white fl. mid-June; bright red berries in clusters. Can be trained as espalier; city hardy; used in hedges.

183. *Pyracantha crenulata*; Crenulated Firethorn. Semi-evgr. shrub. 10°. Small, narrow, serrated, glossy, bright-green, leathery leaves. White fl. in May; orange to red berries in fall. Rusty, pubescent, glabrous branchlets & petioles. (See Plate 271.)

184. *Quercus borealis rubra*; Red Oak. Dec tree. −25°. Tall, rapid growing. City hardy,

Plate 271.   Crenulated Firethorn.
(See plant No. 183.)

Plate 272.   Black Locust.
(See plant No. 197.)

Plate 273.   Weeping Pagoda Tree.
(See plant No. 214.)

Plate 274.   Willow-leaf Spirea.
(See plant No. 220.)

Plate 275.   Thunberg Spirea.
(See plant No. 221.)

185. *Q. coccinea;* Scarlet Oak. Dec. tree. −25°. Tall; bright red leaves in fall.

186. *Q. palustris;* Pin Oak. Dec. tree. −15°. Best in rich, moist soil. Tall; low spreading branches.

187. *Raphiolepsis umbellata;* Yedo Hawthorn; *sharinbai.* Evgr. shrub. 8°. Sun or light shade; hardy in dry, sandy soil. 6'; dark green, thick leaves. White, dense, fragrant fl. late May; blue-black berries fall & winter. Hardy at seashore; used in hedges.

188. *Rhododendron calendulaceum;* Flame Azalea. Dec. shrub, −8°, Acid, moist, cool humus; sun or light shade. 9–12'. Yellow, orange, scarlet fl. early June. Blooms for two weeks; best in North.

189. *R. indicum;* Indian Azalea. Evgr. shrub. 0°. Acid, moist, cool humus; sun or light shade. 6'. Bright red fl. late June.

190. *R. japonicum;* Japanese Azalea; *renge-tsutsuji.* Dec. shrub. −8°. Acid, moist, cool humus; sun or light shade. 6'; hardy, vigorous. Large, red-scarlet fl. late May. Disagreeable smell; therefore plant far from house.

191. *R. keiskei;* Keisk Rhododendron; *hikage-tsutsuji.* Evgr. shrub. −8°. Acid, moist, cool humus; sun or light shade. 9–12'. Yellow, orange, scarlet fl. early June. Blooms for two weeks; best in North.

192. *R. mucronatum;* Snow Azalea; *shiro-ryukyu-tsutsuji.* Evgr. shrub. −8°. Acid. moist, cool humus; sun or light shade. 7'; spreading habit; grayish green leaves. White, fragrant fl. early May.

193. *R. obtusum;* Hiryu Azalea; *Kirishima-tsutsuji.* Semi-evgr. shrub. 0°. Acid, moist, cool humus; sun or light shade. 3'; low, many branches; prostrate habit; autumn leaves reddish. Orange, red fl. mid-May. Best varieties are *hinodegiri* and *kaempferi* or *yamatsutsuji;* city hardy.

194. *Rhodotypos scandens;* Jetbead; *shiro-yamabuki.* Dec. shrub. −8°. Sun or light shade. 6'; low habit. White fl. mid-May; shiny black berries fall & winter. City hardy.

195. *Rhus aromatica;* Fragrant Sumac. Dec. shrub. −25°. Hardy in dry, sandy places. 3'; dense foliage; scarlet in fall. Small, yellow fl. early May; small, red berries summer. Drooping, trailing habit; dio.; hardy in city & near seashore.

196. *R. copallina;* Shining Sumac. Dec. shrub. −15°. Dry soil. 20'; green, glossy leaves turning to scarlet in fall. Crimson, hairy fr. fall through winter. Dio.; hardy in city & near seashore.

197. *Robinia pseudo-acacia;* Black Locust; *harienju, nise-akashia.* Dec. tree. −8°. Hardy in dry, poor soil. 40', narrow; broad at top. Grows rapidly; city hardy. (See Plate 272.)

198. *Rosa chinensis minima;* Fairy Rose; *koshin-bara.* Dec. shrub. 8°. 1'. Rosy red fl. June.

199. *R. laevigata;* Cherokee Rose; *naniwa-ibara.* Dec. shrub. 8°. 15'; thorny. White fragrant fl. May.

200. *R. multiflora;* Japanese Rose; *noi-bara.* Dec. shrub. −8°. 10'; vigorous, thorny, arching. White fl. mid-June; small red berries autumn & winter. City hardy; used in hedge-rows, banks.

201. *R. rugosa;* Rugosa Rose; *hama-nasu.* Dec. shrub. −40°. 6'; dark green leaves turning to orange in fall; thorny. Pink to white fl. early June; red fr. in fall. Hardy in city, seashore; used in hedges; withstands much shearing.

202. *R. wichuraiana;* Memorial Rose; *torihanoi-bara.* Dec. to semi-evgr. −8°. Thorny, procumbent. White fl. mid-July; red fr. Hardy in city, seashore; ground cover for rocky banks & slopes.

203. *Ruscus aculeatus;* Butcher's Broom; *nagiikada.* Evgr. shrub. 8°. Hardy in hot, sun, dry soil, or shade. 2–4'; stiff, low; pointed leathery leaves. Bright red berries winter. Dio.; seashore hardy; needs thinning in spring.

204. *Salix babylonica;* Weeping Willow; *shidare-yanagi.* Dec. tree. −15°. Branches graceful, pendulous; grows fast. Very hardy

in dry, dusty, smoky places as well as wet areas; used in city roof gardens.

205. *S. caprea;* Goat or Pussy Willow. Dec. shrub. Best in moist soil. 25'; vigorous. Composite catkins March. Dio.; cut down every few years to stimulate growth.

206. *Sasa chrysantha;* Aureate Sasa (bamboo). Evgr. in mild winter. 0°. Moist soil. 5'. Spreads by underground rhizomes.

207. *S. palmata;* Senan Sasa (bamboo). Evgr. in mild winter. 0°. Moist soil. 7'; large leaves. Spreads by underground rhizomes.

208. *S. pumila;* Ground Bamboo. Evgr. in mild winter 0°. Moist soil; light shade. 2'; vigorous, spreading. Spreads by underground rhizomes.

209. *S. variegata;* a variety of bamboo. Evgr. in mid winter. 0°. Moist soil. 3'; white striped leaves. Spreads by underground rhizomes.

210. *S. veitchi;* Veitch Sasa. Evgr. in mild winter. 0°. Moist soil 2–4' high; dwarf; running habit. Forms dense foliage mat over ground.

211. *Sciadopitys verticillata;* Umbrella Pine; *koya-maki.* Evgr. tree/shrub. 0°. Hardy in mild winters. 25'; slow growing; dense branches. Best on West Coast and East Coast as far north as N.J.

212. *Semi-arundinaria fastuosa;* Narihira Cane; *narihira-dake.* Evgr. 0°. Moist soil. 15–25'; stately habit. Spreads slowly.

213. *Shibataea kumasasa;* Kumasasa; *bungo-zawa.* Evgr. 0°. Moist soil. 3–6'; low running habit.

214. *Sophora japonica;* Japan Pagoda Tree; *enju.* Dec. tree. −15°. 60'. Yellow-white, long, hanging, panicled fl. Aug. through Sept. Also *Sophora japonica pendula;* Weeping Pagoda Tree; *shidare-enju;* a variety with long, slender, pendulous branches. (See Plate 273.)

215. *S. vicifolia;* Vetch Sophora. Dec. shrub. −8°. Thrives in poor, sandy, dry soil. 7'; arching, graceful habit. Profuse

Plate 276. European Bladdernut.
(See plant No. 222.)

Plate 277. Common Bald Cypress.
(See plant No. 227.)

Plate 278. Hiba False Arbor-vitae.
(See plant No. 230.)

Plate 279. Japanese Torreya.
(See plant No. 232.)

violet to white fl. early June. Thorny stems; feathery leaves.

216. *Sorbus alnifolia;* Korean Mountain Ash. Dec. tree. 50'; upright, dense branching. Small white fl. late May; scarlet berries in fall. Bright green, lustrous leaves, turning scarlet in fall.

217. *Spiraea cantoniensis;* Reeve's Spirea; *kodemari.* Dec. shrub. 0°. Hardy in poor soil; sun or light shade. 3'; spreading habit. White clustered fl. late May. Does best in South and on West Coast.

218. *S. japonica atrosanguinea;* Mikado Spirea. Dec. shrub. −8°. 4'; hardy. Crimson clustered fl. mid-June. Hardy by seashore. Blooms on current year's wood, therefore prune early spring before flowering.

219. *S. prunifolia plena;* Bridal-wreath Spirea. Dec. shrub. −15°. 9'; lustrous, green leaves turning orangish-red in fall. Double white fl. mid-May. Hardy by seashore. Blooms on previous year's wood, therefore prune after flowering.

220. *S. salicifolia;* Willow-leaf Spirea; *hozakinoshimotsuke.* Dec. shrub. −15°. Hardy in wet soil. 4'; rigid, standing habit. Rose-colored, spiked fl. early June. Hardy by seashore; spreads by suckers. (See Plate 274.)

221. *S. thunbergi;* Thunberg Spirea; *yukiyanagi.* Dec. shrub. −15°. 5'; arching, thin, feathery branches; leaves turn orange to yellow in autumn. Small white fl. late Apl., early May. Requires pruning out of dead twigs; hardy in city, by seashore, roof gardens; blooms on previous year's wood. (See Plate 275.)

222. *Staphylea pinnata;* European Bladdernut. Dec. shrub. −5°. Upright habit; light green leaves; pinkish white fl. in nodding clusters in May-June; inflated, bladderlike fr. Prefers moist, rich earth and partial shade. (See Plate 276.)

223. *Stewartia pseudocamellia;* Japanese Stewartia: *natsu-tsubaki.* Dec. shrub. −8°. 25'; bright green leaves turning purple in fall. White fl. early July.

224. *Styrax japonica;* Japanese Snowball. Dec. shrub. −8°. 25'; dense, spreading, curving, lateral branches. White, bell-shaped, pendulous fl. early June.

225. *Syringa amurensis japonica;* Japanese Tree Lilac; *hashidoi.* Dec. shrub. −15°. Generally hardy in most situations. 25'; vigorous. White fl. mid-June. Cherrylike bark; city & seashore hardy; used in hedges & screens. All lilacs need regular pruning.

226. *S. vulgaris;* Common Lilac. Dec. shrub. −25°. Generally hardy. 20'; dense, upright, vigorous. Fragrant fl. mid-May. City hardy; used in hedges; prune suckers; many varieties of this species.

227. *Taxodium distichum;* Common Bald Cypress. Dec. Tree. −15°. Hardy as far north as Boston but generally smaller in north. Common in swampy areas from Delaware to Texas, reaching 150' height. Feathery, needlelike, light foliage appearing in late spring. Spreading, upright habit; cones one inch long. (See Plate 277.)

228. *Taxus cuspidata (aurescens, densa, expansa, nana);* Japanese Yew (yellow, dense, open, dwarf); *ichii, onko, kyaraboku.* Evgr. shrub. −15°. Generally hardy in cold or drought, sun, or shade. 4-40'; rich, green needles; some varieties upright, spreading, dwarf; picturesque branching. Red, fleshy berries autumn. Withstands much shearing and pruning; good in hedges; slow growing; compact habit; city & seashore hardy; used in roof gardens; dio.

229. *Thuja occidentalis;* American Arborvitae. Evgr. shrub tree. −40°. Needs moist, rich soil. 35'; scalelike foliage. Protect from sun scorching; used as foundation planting; sheared hedges.

230. *Thujopsis dolabrata;* Hiba False Arborvitae; *hiba.* Evgr. tree. 0°. A conifer; 50'. Pyramidal habit. Frondlike branches. Prefers sheltered, shady locations & moist, loamy soil & cool, moist climate. Hardy to Massachusetts. (See Plate 278.)

231. *Tsuga canadensis;* Common Hemlock. Evgr. tree −15°. Sun or partial shade. 90', but may be pruned to hedge heights. Lustrous dark green needles; withstands much pruning; used in hedges & wind breaks.

232. *Torreya nucifera;* Japanese Torreya; *kaya.* Evgr. tree. −5°. Pyramidal compact head, spreading habit; 75'. Bright red bark; lanceolate, yew-like foliage. Prefers shady, sheltered location; moist, loamy soil. Fr. drupelike and edible. Dio. (See Plate 279.)

233. *Vaccinium corymbosum;* Highbush Blueberry. Dec. shrub. −25°. Best in acid soil; sun or shade. 12'; vigorous, dense; leaves turn scarlet in fall. White, pink fl. late May; blue, black edible berries summer & early fall. Hardy in city; red twigs in winter.

234. *Viburnum sieboldi;* Siebold Viburnum. Dec. shrub. −20°. Does well in shade. 30'; dark green, lustrous leaves turn red in fall. White clustered fl. late May; red & black berries on red stalks in summer. Hardy in city, roof gardens, at seashore; fragrant leaves.

235. *V. tomentosum mariesi;* Maries Double-file Viburnum; *odemari, temari-bana.* Dec. shrub. −15°. 9'; lateral branches; leaves turn red in fall. White, flat, clustered fl. late May; red berries in fall. City hardy.

236. *Weigela "Bristol Ruby";* Weigela. Dec. shrub. −15°. 5'. Dark red fl. mid-May. Hybrid; city hardy.

237. *Zelkova serrata;* Japanese Zelkova; *keyaki.* Dec. tree. −8°. 85'; top round; short trunk, many vertical branches. Good substitute for American elm; fine shade; yellow to brown leaves in fall.

Bibliography

On Japanese Gardens

Amanuma, Shinichi; Shigemori, Mirei; and Nakano, Sokei (eds.): *Teien: Kyoto Bijutsu Taikan* (Gardens: Kyoto Art Survey). Tokyo, 1933.

Kitao, Harumichi: *Satei* (Teahouse Gardens). Shokokusha, Tokyo, 1954.

Kubo, Tadashi: "An Oldest Note of Secrets on Japanese Gardens: A Compilation of the 'Sakutei-ki'." *Bulletin of Osaka Prefectural University*, Series B, Vol. 6, 1956.

Kuck, Loraine E.: *The Art of Japanese Gardens*. John Day, New York, 1940.

——: *One Hundred Kyoto Gardens*. Thompson (Bunkado), Kobe, 1936.

Newsom, Samuel: *A Thousand Years of Japanese Gardens*. Tokyo News Service, Tokyo, 1953.

Nishimura, Tei: *Niwa to Chashitsu* (Gardens and Teahouses). Kodansha, Tokyo, 1957.

Rito, Akisato: *Shinsen Teizo Den* (Report on a New Selection of Gardens). 1828.

——: *Tsukiyama Teizo Den* (Report on the Building of Artificial-Hill Gardens). 1828.

Saito, Katsuo: *Niwa Tsukuri* (Garden Making). Gihodo, Tokyo, 1955.

——: *Sho Teien* (The Small Garden). Kawade Shobo, Tokyo, 1954.

Shigemori, Kanto: *Nihon no Teien Geijutsu* (Artistic Gardens of Japan), 3 v. Riko Tosho, Tokyo, 1957.

Shigemori, Mirei: *Kinki Meien no Kansho* (An Appreciation of Noted Gardens in the Kinki Region). Kyoto Inshokan, Kyoto, 1946.

Takakuwa, Gisei: *Gardens of Japan*. Suiko Shoin, Kyoto, 1958.

Tamura, Tsuyoshi: *Art of the Landscape Garden in Japan*. Trans. by Sumie Mishima. Kokusai Bunka Shinkokai, Tokyo, 1947.

——: *Jardin Japonais: Ses Origines et Caracteres, Dessins et Plans*. Kokusai Bunka Shinkokai, Tokyo, 1939.

Tatsui, Matsunosuke: *Japanese Gardens*. Japan Travel Bureau, Tokyo, 1956.

Tsumura, Hideo: *Nippon Teien Shu* (A Collection of Japanese Gardens). Kodani Shobo, Osaka, 1955.

Yoshinaga, Yoshinobu: *Nihon no Teien* (Japanese Traditional Gardens). Shokokusha, Tokyo, 1958.

On Related Japanese Subjects

Horiguchi, Sutemi: *Katsura Rikyu* (Katsura Imperial Villa). Mainichi, Tokyo, 1957.

Murasaki Shikibu, Lady: *The Tale of Genji: A Novel in Six Parts*. Trans. by Arthur Waley. Allen & Unwin, London, 1935.

Niwa, Teizo: *Katsura Rikyu no Tobi-ishi* (Steppingstones of the Katsura Imperial Villa). Shokokusha, Tokyo, 1955.

Okakura, Kakuzo (Tenshin): *The Book of Tea*. Tuttle, Tokyo & Rutland, 1956.

Taniguchi, Yoshiro: *Shugaku-in Rikyu* (Shugaku-in Imperial Villa). Mainichi, Tokyo, 1956.

Usami, Kanji: *Sukiya Gonomi* (Sukiya-Style Garden Structures). Yachio Shoin, Tokyo, 1955.

Yoshimura, Yuji, and Halford, Giovanna M.: *The Japanese Art of Miniature Trees and Landscapes: Their Creation, Care, and Enjoyment*. Tuttle, Tokyo & Rutland, 1957.

On Landscape Design

Church, Thomas D.: *Gardens Are for People*. Reinhold, New York, 1955.

Eckbo, Garrett: *Landscape for Living*. Architectural Record Book, Dodge, New York, 1950.

Hubbard, Henry Vincent, and Kimball, Theodora: *An Introduction to the Study of Landscape Design*. Macmillan, New York, 1924.

Rose, James: *Creative Gardens.* Reinhold, New York, 1958.

Tunnard, Christopher: *Gardens in the Modern Landscape.* Architectural Press, London, and Scribner's, New York; 1948.

On Plant Materials

Bailey, L. H., and the staff of the Bailey Hortorium, Cornell University: *Manual of Cultivated Plants Most Commonly Grown in the Continental United States and Canada.* Macmillan, New York, 1939.

Kelsey, Harlan P., and Dayton, William A. (Editorial Board of American Joint Committee on Horticultural Nomenclature): *Standardized Plant Names.* J. Horace McFarland Co.; Harrisburg, Pa.; 1942.

Levison, J. J.: *The Home Book of Trees and Shrubs.* Knopf, New York, 1949.

Wyman, Donald: *Ground Cover Plants.* Macmillan, New York, 1950.

——: *Shrubs and Vines for American Gardens.* Macmillan, New York, 1953.

——: *Trees for American Gardens.* Macmillan, New York, 1956.

Index

Note: References are to page numbers and, following a decimal point, to specific items (plates, figures, or plant numbers) appearing on those pages. Thus the reference 247.1 is to the item numbered 1 on page 247. In the case of a color plate, the number of the *facing* page is given as the reference, in italics. Scientific names of plants, not included here, are arranged alphabetically on pages 247–63.

abelia, glossy, 247.1
acanthopanax, 247.8
actinidia, bower, 249.13
age and antiquity, 9, 27
ajisai, 255.99
akebi, 249.14
akebia, five-leaf, 249.14
alder, black, 255.105
almond, dwarf flowering, 259.168
andromeda, Japanese, 259.159
aoki, 249.22
arborvitae: American, 263.229; hiba false, 263.230
ardisia, coral, 249.18
Art of the Japanese Garden, The, 24
artificial-hill garden, 19–20
asebi, 259.159
ash, Korean mountain, 263.216
asymmetry, 13, 26, 27
aucuba, Japanese, 249.22
azalea: flame, 261.188; hiryu 261.193; Indian, 261.189; Japanese, 261.190; Keisk rhododendron, 261.191; snow, 261.192

bamboo, 27, 81.32, 82.33, 110.67; arrow, 259.179; aureate sasa, 261.206; grass, 249.16; golden, 259.156; ground, 261.208; kumasasa, 261.213; metake, 259.179; misc., 261.209; narihira cane, 261.212; senan sasa, 261.207; Simon, 249.17; timber, 259.157; Veitch sasa, 261.210; *see also* fences
banana shrub, 257.140
baran, 249.21
barberry: cutleaf, 249.24; Japanese, 249.27; Korean, 249.25; Mentor, 249.26; paleleaf, 249.23
basins, stone, 30, 42–43, 203–15.185–201
bay, sweet, 255.120
bayberry, 257.142
beauty-berry, Japanese, 249.33
beauty bush, 255.116

binan-kazura, 255.113
birch: American gray, 249.31; paper, 249.30; sweet, 249.28; white, 249.30; yellow, 249.29
bittersweet: American, 251.39; Oriental 249.38
bladdernut, European, 263.222
blueberry, highbush, 263.233
boat landings, 128–29, 90–92
boke, 251.45
Book of Tea, The, 13.20, 21
botan, 257.149
box: Japanese, Korean, little-leaf, 249.32
box sand-myrtle, 255.121
bridges, 43–44, 219.207, 222–33.210–25
broom: butcher's, 261.203; Scotch, 253.77
Buddhism, 12, 17
bungo-zawa, 261.213
bush-clover: Japanese, 255.123; shrub, 255.122
bussoge, 255.97
byakushin, 255.108

camellia; common, 249.34; sasanqua, 249.35
cane, *see* bamboo
care of garden, 46–50
cast iron plant, 249.21
cedar: deodar, 249.37; eastern red, 255.112
cha-niwa (tea garden), 20–21
cherry: double Chinese flowering, 259.175; Japanese flowering, 259.169, 259.171; Manchu, 259.178; Nakai Chinese bush, 259.170; Nippon, 259.173; Sargent, 259.174; victory flowering, 259.176; weeping higan, 259.177
Chinzan-so, 168.138, 180.152, 181.153, 242.235
chiri-ana (dust-hole), 97.52
Chisaku-in, 224.212, 230.222
chosen-goyo, 259.161
chosen-maki, 251.40
chosen-matsu, 259.161
chozubachi (water basin), 30
classifications of gardens, 19–21

clematis: pink anemone, 251.58; sweet autumn, 251.59
clethra, Japanese, 251.61
color, in garden design, 13–14
cornel, Japanese, 251.65
cosmology, 17
courtyard garden, 100.56
crab-apple: cutleaf, 257.139; Japanese flowering, 257.136; Sargent, 257.138; Toringo, 257.137
crape myrtle, 255.118
cryptomeria, 253.73
cypress: common bald, 263.227; Monterey, 253.75
cypress, Sawara false: midget, 251.53; moss, 251.56; thread, 251.54

Daikaku-ji, 216.202
Daisen-in, 62.11, 159.129, 234.226
Daitoku-ji, 65.15, 79.30, 174.145, 185.157, 237.230
daphne, winter, 253.78
deutzia, slender, 253.79
dodan-tsutsuji 253.82
dogwood: Japanese, 251.64; Japanese cornel, 251.65; Siberian, 251.62; white flowering, 251.63
drainage, 26
"dry landscape," 20, 62.11, 119–21.78–80
dust-hole, 97.52

Eckbo, Garrett, 11
elaeagnus, cherry, 253.80
enclosures, 34–39
enishida, 253.77
enju, 261.214
enkianthus: red-vein, 253.81; white, 253.82
Enri-an, 147.113, 158.127, 165.135
eulalia, 257.141
euonymus: evergreen, 253.85; Yedo, 253.86
eurya, Japanese, 253.88

leucothoe: drooping, 255.124; Keisk's, 255.125
lilac: common, 263.226; Japanese tree, 263.225
line and mass, in garden design, 13–14
locust, black, 261.197

maackia, 257.132
magnolia: purple lily, 257.133; star, 257.134
mahonia, leatherleaf, 257.135
maiden-hair tree, 253.95
Manpuku-ji, 169.139
manryo, 249.18
Manshu-in, 119.78, 214.198
maple: Amur, 247.9; Japanese, 247.10; red, 247.11; sugar, 249.12
marshes, 32
masaki, 253.85
mass, in garden design, 13–14, 26–27
mokuren, 257.133
mokusei, 257.146
momiji, 247.10
moods, garden, 21
moss, 9.4, 56.3, 85.36, 87.38, 92.44, 134.98
Moss Temple; *see* Saiho-ji
mountainous feeling, how achieved, 26
mukuge, 255.98
Murasaki, Lady, 14
murasaki-shikibu, 249.33
Murin-an, 122.82, 192.166, 194.170
Muso Kokushi, *5.2*
Myoshin-ji, 185.158
mystery, garden effect of, 26, 58.5

nagiikada, 261.203
nandina, 65.14, 257.143
naniwa-ibara, 261.199
nanten, 257.143
Nanzen-ji, 172.142–43, 235.227–28
narihira-dake, 261.212
natsu-tsubaki, 263.223
naturalism, humanized, 12–13
nezumi-mochi, 126.88
nise-akashia, 261.197
nobedan, see pavements
noi-bara, 261.200
nozen-kazura, 249.36
noren (doorway curtain), 77.28

oak: pin, 261.186; red, 259.184; scarlet, 261.185

obai, 255.107
Obai-in, 213.197
obaiibota, 257.128
odemari, 263.235
Okakura, Kakuzo, 13, 20–21
oleander, 257.144
onko, 263.228
orange, mock, 257.152
oribe lantern style, 76.26–27, 111.68, 199–200.179–81
osmanthus: Fortune, 257.145; fragrant, 257.146; golden, 257.146; holly, 257.147

pachysandra, 257.148
pagoda tree: Japan, 261.214; weeping, 261.214
pagodas; *see* towers
Paradise, Island of, 14, 19
paths, *25.13–14*
pavements, 40–41, 82.33, 94.48, 108.65, 175.146, 177–91.148–65; *see also* stepping-stones
pebbles, as groundcover, 81.32
peony, tree, 257.149
perspective, garden, 24–26
pine: eastern white, 259.164; Japanese black, 259.165; Japanese white, 259.163; Korean, 259.161; Mugo, 259.162; tanyosho, 259.160; umbrella, 261.211
pine trees, 242.235–36; pruning, 47.63, 48.64, 49
pittisporum, Japanese, 259.166
planning of garden, 23–26
plum, beach, 259.172
podocarpus, shrubby yew, 259.167
pomegranate, 259.181
ponds, *4.1, 5.2,* 32, 118.76–77; shorelines of, 129–34.92–98
pottery, 39
privacy, garden, 8–9
privet: border, 257.127; California, 257.128; Japanese, 255.126; Regel, 257.127
pruning, 46–49, 58.5, 72.22, 73.23, 78.29, 86.37, 103.59–60, 243.237
purple cup, 257.152

quince: flowering, 251.45; Japanese, 251.44

Raiko-ji, *21.11*
rakuyoso, 255.119

redbud, eastern, 251.42
renge-tsutsuji, 261.190
rengyo, 253.92
rhythm, nature's, 9
robai, 251.57
rocks, use of, 17–18, 24–29
rockspray, 253.69; Sungari, 253.70
Rokuo-in, 242.236
rose: Cherokee, 261.199; fairy, 261.198; Japanese, 261.200; memorial, 261.202; Rugosa, 261.201
Ryoan-ji, 18, 20, 61.10, 139.104, 186.159, 211.193, 231.223
ryobu, 251.61

sabi, 21, 27, 52
sage brush, fringed, 249.19
sago cycas, 253.76
Saiho-ji, *8.3, 9.4,* 63.12, 134.98, 154.122
St. Johnswort: Henry, 255.102; Hooker's, 255.101
Sakutei-ki, 31–33
Sambo-in, *45.16,* 118.76
sand: gravelly, 44, 82.33; patterns in, 44, 102.58, 159.129, 234–40.226–33
Sano, Tansai, *13.6–7, 21.10,* 198.177
sanshuyu, 251.65
sanzashi, 253.71
sarasadodan, 253.81
saru-suberi, 255.118
sasa; *see* bamboo
sato-zakura, 259.175
sashide, 48
sawara, 251.53
sazanka, 249.35
scale, of a garden, 24
scouring rush, 253.83
sculpture, 43, 56.3, 68.18, 84.35, **113.70,** 216–17.202–5
Seiren-in, 203.185, 219.207
seiyo-hinoki, 253.75
sekimori-ishi, 41.60
serviceberry, Asian, 249.15
shadbush, 249.15
shakkei, 34
sharinbai, 261.187
shidare-enju, 261.214
shidare-yanagi, 261.204
shidare-zakura, 259.177
shide-kobushi, 257.134
shimokuren, 257.133
shin style, 21